Illustration by Harold Riley

KARSTEN'S
WAY

KARSTEN'S WAY

The Life-Changing Story of
Karsten Solheim— Pioneer in Golf
Club Design and the Founder of PING®

TRACY SUMNER

NORTHFIELD PUBLISHING
CHICAGO

©2000 by
THE SOLHEIM FOUNDATION

All Scripture quotations are taken from the King James Version.

ISBN: 1-881273-14-8

1 3 5 7 9 10 8 6 4 2

Printed in the United States of America

To the employees of
Karsten Manufacturing Corporation

CONTENTS

FOREWORD

Karsten Solheim was many things: a devoted family man, a man of great faith, an engineer by training, an habitual inventor, and, as a result, an innovator and visionary in matters both large and small. He also was a very humble person. While he achieved financial success during his lifetime, and no small amount of fame in the game of golf, he was never motivated by money or notoriety but instead by the desire to make golf easier for people. His simple desire to make a better putter caused a revolution in the world of golf that resulted in the creation of countless new standards for golf equipment.

However, his legacy will be far more than having created new standards within the golf industry. Karsten was about people . . . his family, his employees, his customers, his friends . . . not only helping them improve their golf game but also their lives. His financial success enabled him and his family to establish previously unheard of benchmarks in giving back to the game of golf and people and organizations in need. Who knows the countless number of times he provided financial assistance for a struggling student or golf pro, underwrote the cost of a program or building, or assisted someone in achieving a dream?

I consider myself very lucky to have known Karsten Solheim. The Ladies Professional Golf Association (LPGA), of which I am the commissioner, celebrated its 50th anniversary in 2000. Karsten's support of the LPGA for more than half of our 50-year history was one of the biggest, if not the biggest, reason the LPGA has achieved its status as the most successful women's professional sports organization in the world. I am hard pressed to think of anyone who has done more to help women's professional golf than Karsten Solheim.

As he was in most things, Karsten was a trailblazer in women's golf, and he backed his beliefs with action. He believed that women golfers deserved the same opportunities as their male counterparts, and he put that belief into action through co-sponsoring tournaments, supporting literally hundreds of LPGA players over the years, and starting The Solheim Cup.

The Solheim Cup, one of the most special events in all of women's professional golf, is the result of Karsten's dreams for enriching women's golf. Founded by Karsten and his family in 1990, The Solheim Cup in just 10 years has evolved into the preeminent international competition in women's golf. Known as the women's version of the Ryder Cup, The Solheim Cup showcases the best U.S.-born golfers from the LPGA and the top European-born players on the Evian Tour, the women's European golf tour. The memories and poignant moments from the five Solheim Cups are among the most treasured by all the players who have been fortunate enough to compete.

To list these contributions illustrates Karsten's commitment to women's golf and his impact on the golf industry, but they don't truly illustrate the man . . . his genius, his integrity, his loyalty, his vision. I believe Ralph Waldo Emerson's definition of success best describes Karsten and his way.

> ". . . to laugh often and much; to win the respect of intelligent people and affection of children; to earn the appreciation of honest critics and endure the betrayal of false friends; to appreciate beauty, to find the best in others; to leave the world a bit better, whether by a healthy child, a garden patch *(and with apologies to Emerson, a better putter),* or a redeemed social condition; to know even one life has breathed easier because you have lived. This is to have succeeded."

Karsten Solheim more than succeeded . . . he changed the world of golf, and we are all the better for having known him. Women's golf has had no greater angel than Karsten Solheim, and the game of golf has never seen a greater innovator. He will be sorely missed, but his legacy will live on in the hearts and minds of us all.

TY M. VOTAW
Commissioner
Ladies Professional Golf Association
June 2000

INTRODUCTION

 H ow did your husband get started in the golf business?" is a question I have been asked more times than I can remember. Answering that question is never simple and usually leads to more questions, most of which I try to answer as concisely as I can. But the end result is almost always the same: the person questioning will say, "What an interesting story! Someone should put that into a book!"

I didn't pay much attention to that for many years, because Karsten's achievements in the golf industry were being written up in so many periodicals—all the sports magazines, especially those on golf, and many others as well.

But these journalists and feature writers were all missing a vital part of the real Karsten that I knew so well. I couldn't fault them; I would be at a loss to put into words that spiritual essence of my husband. As the years went by, and I was continually confronted by the question of when was a book going to be written about him, I continued to pass it off.

When the decision was finally made to write a book in early 1996, I contacted Dr. Joseph Stowell, President of Moody Bible Institute in Chicago, and asked for help. We had gotten acquainted with Dr. Stowell nearly ten years earlier when the Solheim Center was being constructed for Moody. One son and five of our ten grandchildren have attended MBI, and three of them are graduates. Joe put me in contact with Greg Thornton, Vice President of Publications at the Institute, and finally the book got underway.

It was too late for one vital need—Karsten's personal input. His Parkinson's disease had progressed to a point where it was very difficult for him to communicate. And when I told him someone was there to interview him for a book, he refused to take part, saying, "I don't want a book written about me!" However, having put my hand to the plow, I decided to see the project through.

What was it that set Karsten Solheim apart from the average man? He was a simple man, with simple tastes. When at the age of nearly fifty-six he incorporated his growing golf business, he decided right away that even though he was its president, he would not come to work in a suit and tie. He had had at least twenty-five years of that and that was enough; he would wear a golf shirt and slacks. Jewelry didn't interest him at all. He didn't wear a wedding ring, saying it might get caught in the machinery. Watches had to be plain and serviceable. He met a tailor in a Hong Kong hotel on our first trip there in 1967 and depended on him to provide the clothes he needed for the next thirty years. He was not fussy about his food either, preferring restaurants that had plain food and fast service. His favorite meal was a baked potato, fish such as salmon or shrimp, and soup, split pea perhaps. Dessert was his weakness, and apple pie à la mode was special to him.

His simple way of dressing did not camouflage who was in charge at either KMC or any of the subsidiaries. George Ball, for many years the general manager of Dolphin, Inc., our investment-casting foundry, tells the story of Karsten's bringing a carful of Japanese visitors to the foundry one day. They had already spent a day or so visiting the golf factory, and Karsten was himself driving them to the airport. Karsten looked at his watch and decided they had time to make a quick visit to the foundry.

A new girl was at the receptionist's desk and was taken aback at Karsten's request for an immediate tour—also his asking if they were doing any pouring. (Pouring the red-hot molten metal into the lost wax ceramic castings is always a spectacular process.) The girl excused herself for a moment and rushed into George's office, saying, "There's a bunch of Japanese in the lobby wanting a tour, and the one with a beard acts like he owns the place!"

George smiled at the girl, "Let's see what we can do for them. The Japanese with the beard does own the place!"

Karsten was also a complicated man; if his mind jumped ahead from mountaintop to mountaintop while the rest of us were plodding up the hills, down into the valleys, and up another hill, so be it. I discovered early on that usually what he had in mind was better than anything I dreamed of and was worth the waiting.

A few years ago we were in England and were having tea with a group of new friends. Striving to make conversation with the lady next to me, I mentioned that we had just celebrated our fifty-fourth wedding anniversary. "Fifty-four years to the same man?" she responded. "How boring!" In all, Karsten and I had sixty-three years and eight months together, and it was anything but boring!

Karsten really had four successful careers: when we were married, he had been running his own shoe repair shop for four years, and he continued doing that for the next four years. Then he went into selling, putting on demonstration dinners for waterless cookware called Miracle Maid, hiring and training salesmen. Though interrupted by World War Two, he did this for nine years. Next came his career as an engineer, which totaled eighteen years, the last eight coinciding with the first eight years of our fledgling golf company. Karsten loved whatever he was doing, but designing, manufacturing, and selling golf clubs was his best. As long as he was able to go to work, he greeted each new day with a zest and enthusiasm that inspired us all.

After Karsten's death on February 16, 2000, we were overwhelmed by the outpouring of love, respect, and fond memories from people all over the world. It is comforting to know that Karsten's life touched so many people. I count it a privilege to have shared that life with him.

LOUISE SOLHEIM

1

KARSTEN'S WAY

The Man Who Changed the Golf Club Industry

H e's been called a visionary, a revolutionary, a genius. He has been credited in some circles with virtually inventing the modern game of golf—or at least with so indelibly stamping his mark on the golf equipment industry that scarcely a club made today doesn't in some way bear a resemblance to the clubs he designed. He's been seen as an outsider in the golf-club industry and a maverick in the way he ran his business—from how he treated his employees to how he built and marketed his products. He is known as a man who knew how to solve problems, no matter how simple or complicated they may be.

Whatever adjectives you apply to the man, whatever changes in the golf equipment industry you credit him with, and no matter how you describe him, there's no question that Karsten Solheim forever changed the face of golf and the golf equipment business. He left his imprint on the equipment golfers at all levels of competition use to play their sport. And he revolutionized the way golf manufacturers produce and market their products.

It's rare at the beginning of the twenty-first century to find a piece of golf equipment that doesn't owe at least part of its design to Karsten Solheim. Golf manufacturers have been using his ideas—at least variations of them—for a generation, and since many of the patents on Karsten's clubs have long run out, much of the new equipment are blatant copies or knockoffs of what Karsten Manufacturing has been doing from the beginning. Ideas such as heel-toe and perimeter weighting, investment casting, and custom fitting—all pivotal in the development of Karsten Solheim's clubs—are now in use in many quarters of the golf equipment industry. It has been estimated that there are literally hundreds of duplicates and clones of Ping's Anser putter alone on the market today.

It's an impressive story, especially when you consider that it is the story of a man who never played golf until he was in his early forties but who went on to become one of the most important figures in the game.

LOOKING FOR SOLUTIONS

As the inventor of Ping golf clubs and the founder and president of Karsten Manufacturing, which builds and markets Ping clubs, Karsten Solheim was nothing if not a problem solver. He was truly a visionary whose goal was to make things better for golfers at all levels of the game. From the beginning of his involvement in golf-club manufacturing in the late 1950s, Karsten Solheim set about solving a problem that all golfers know about: equipment that made the game more difficult than it needed to be, equipment that was so unforgiving that it required near perfection on the part of golfers in order to turn in a decent score. As far as Karsten was concerned, there were enough variables in the game of golf already—the weather, the course, the golfer himself or herself—without the golfer's having to battle his or her equipment. So he looked at the problem, then found a way to solve it.

Karsten Solheim's brilliant mind could examine a problem, figure out what caused the problem, then work to make the necessary corrections. From the time he began playing golf, he had the unique ability to look at his own shortcomings and those of other golfers at all levels and figure out how changes in equipment could help the golfer become the best he or she could be. In other words, Karsten wanted to design golf clubs that were an asset and not an actual hindrance to a golfer's game.

The results speak for themselves. The Ping golf clubs—the putters, the irons, and the woods—are among the most popular in the world, and certain models have maintained their place as the best-selling clubs in their classification. The Ping Anser putter, first produced in 1966, wasn't Karsten's first putter, but it was by far the most successful. Modeled after his original putters with some improvements, the Anser has played a part in more than 500 professional tournament victories worldwide and is considered the all-time best-selling putter. The Titleist Bulls Eye, the Wilson 8802, and the Ram Zebra are extremely popular putters and rightly so, but the consensus among industry experts is that the Anser is the best-selling ever.

With Ping's spot in the putter market firmly established, Karsten moved on in the early '60s to designing and manufacturing irons. The results were no less spectacular. Ping's Eye2, first introduced in 1982, is the single most popular iron ever created. More sets of the Eye2 were sold than any other iron, and they are still being made.

A DIFFERENT MOTIVATION

Karsten Solheim's ideas made him a wealthy man, but he never had as his motivation the pursuit of worldly riches. Karsten was a complex man, who was in many ways a contradiction to most self-made millionaires. He was a man who never set out to make a fortune but only to earn a comfortable living for his family and to help golfers at all levels to improve their games. He did not spend his life in the pursuit of money. In his life and his business, Karsten never pursued profits and riches.

To Karsten Solheim, money was nothing more than a means to make other people's lives more comfortable. He was a man who was concerned first with people. He enjoyed using his know-how—and it was know-how that seemingly came naturally, as you will see later on—to help golfers hit the ball straighter and to allow the thousands of people who worked for him over the years to earn a good living so that they and their families could live comfortable lives.

Karsten Solheim's ability to solve problems made him wealthy indeed, but it also helped some of the greatest golfers of all time to etch their names into the history of the sport.

DOING IT HIS WAY

Karsten Solheim ran his business under the philosophy that if you don't constantly improve, you will stagnate and be overtaken by the competition. That showed itself in how Karsten Manufacturing expanded, first from putters to irons, then from irons to woods, then from woods to all sorts of golf equipment and accessories, including bags, clothing, and, for a time, golf balls.

Most businessmen who have enjoyed this kind of success have resorted to mass marketing, mass production, and price discounting to enjoy the kind of volume Karsten

Manufacturing has enjoyed. But Karsten Solheim had other ideas, which made his Phoenix-based conglomerate a model in the business world. He never discounted or mass marketed. Rather, he manufactured products at the highest level possible and trusted the discriminating buyer to rise to the appropriate price. Every piece was custom-made, one at a time, to fill a standing order.

Karsten's way was simple: Build it better, sell it at a fair price (fair to the producer as well as the consumer), and let the quality of the product speak for itself. That way of doing business was a successful one too, and many of the game's top tour players had a hand in making Ping the success that it has become.

From the time Julius Boros became the first professional golfer to win a tour event, the 1967 Phoenix Open, using a Cushin model Ping putter, some of the biggest names in the world of professional golf—Tom Watson, Seve Ballesteros, Nick Faldo, and Paul Azinger on the men's tour, and Betsy Rawls, JoAnne Carner, Beth Daniel, and Judy Rankin on the women's tour, to name a few—have given Karsten's putters a great deal of credit for their success.

While Karsten owed much of his success to the professional golfers who used his products and were successful with them, he also enjoyed helping even the most rank amateur golfer improve by using his clubs. From the very beginning, his goal was to use his giftedness to make golf easier for people. With an improved club, golfers at all levels play better, enjoy the game more, and derive more satisfaction from it. Karsten loved the idea of making golf more fun for those who play the game, and he loved to hear from those who liked his clubs.

There was nothing Karsten Solheim enjoyed more than meeting people who used his equipment and improved their golf games as a result. He always had time for people. He loved being approached by people—on golf courses, in airports, in restaurants, wherever he would meet them—who wanted to thank him for his innovations in the game. He was approached often by people wanting his autograph, wanting to talk to him, or wanting to have their picture taken with him. And almost without fail, he accommodated their requests. He always took time to talk to the customers who liked his products. He was even known to miss flights in order to spend time with people who wanted to talk to him.

Karsten Solheim was, in many people's eyes, the ideal boss. He worked to make sure that the thousands who worked in the Karsten Manufacturing plant loved their jobs, knew him personally, were free to address him as "Karsten," and were paid well enough to provide a comfortable life for their families. He did that not just because he wanted his employees to work harder for him, but also because he knew it would make them happier people.

While many businessmen might balk at his ways of doing business, it's hard to argue with the results. Karsten Solheim was an incredible success, both in terms of finances and human relations. He was, in every objectively measurable way, a true self-made success story. Karsten would say only, "God blessed us."

AN UNLIKELY SUCCESS STORY

Anyone looking to grow and excel in his or her own business would do well to study the life of golf's genius, to take a long look at the man whose old-world values—hard work, unflinching honesty and integrity, and a deep-seated sense of loyalty—made him what he became in the modern business world. On every level of his business, this Norwegian-born engineer, designer, and salesman is an icon to any armchair thinker who ever dreamed of an idea that would make his fortune. The man who reached such heights in the second half of his life did not come to corporate America through an MBA program. Rather, Karsten Solheim was an unlikely genius, an outsider in the world of golf who made his fortune through the kind of hard work and perseverance rarely seen in today's business world. Most everybody who knew Karsten Solheim knew him as a good man: a humanitarian, a philanthropist, an honest and loyal businessman, a tireless worker, and a man who loved his wife and his children. But he was not a perfect man. He dealt with all his associates honestly, but he had his enemies in the business world. He believed deeply in the importance of the family and loved his own, but he had his shortcomings as a husband and father. And for those who found him inspirational and a catalyst for creative thinking, there were others who saw him as rigid, stubborn, and impatient. Even those who respected and loved him the most say with a smile, "It always had to be Karsten's way." In short, as with so many, his strengths were also his weaknesses.

But a look into the past of Karsten Solheim reveals much about what made him the man that he became. It reveals much about his professional and personal ways, about what shaped his personality, his business, and his family. An overview of his surprising past sheds light on the crucible of endurance necessary to produce such results. His principles of business, management, marketing, manufacturing, and even personal growth were forged and refined in the fire of real life.

The man who owned the manufacturing plant now run by his sons in Phoenix, Arizona, and who became a giant in the world of golf didn't have the kind of early life you would expect for someone of his stature. He didn't grow up in a life of privilege. He was, in fact, a motherless child.

2

AGAINST ALL ODDS

The Unlikely Shaping of a Genius

Considering Karsten Solheim's personal history, particularly his upbringing, it's amazing that he made anything of his life, let alone that he became a legendary success in the world of business. He didn't come from an advantaged background. In fact, he grew up without his mother and, for a crucial time in his early childhood, without his father, facing untold sadness and disadvantage as a young child.

Today, the kind of upbringing Karsten endured is routinely used as an excuse for all sorts of antisocial behavior and dysfunction. It might seem understandable in our modern culture to expect a man such as Karsten never to amount to much by the world's standards. But Karsten Solheim came along in an era when childhood trauma was no excuse for adult dysfunction. He grew up in an era when that sort of disadvantage was a source of personal strength and fortitude.

Those who knew Karsten Solheim well understood that he was a good man with flaws, and that, despite his love for people, he struggled with interpersonal relationships. But to accurately perceive this complex man—his strengths, his weaknesses, his flaws—you must look into his past. In order to understand his successes and failures in business, as an employer and as a husband and father, you have to look at the man through the window of a very difficult background. With that factor in mind, it is possible to understand how Karsten Solheim became what he became, professionally and personally, as an inventor, businessman, employer, and husband and father.

Understanding Karsten Solheim's background gives understanding of his personality, which many have seen as hardheaded, stubborn, aloof, and noncommunicative. But it also makes it all the easier to admire the man who rose from nothing to become one of the most important figures in late-twentieth-century golf. It helps us to understand a man who, despite his shortcomings, was also a humanitarian who had a deep love for people. It helps us to admire more the genius of Karsten Solheim.

A MOTHERLESS CHILD

Karsten Solheim's birth certificate says he was born in Bergen, Norway, on September 14, 1911, a firstborn. But for some reason, the family always celebrated his birthday as September 15. His father, Helleman Andreas Solheim, was a shoemaker like his own father. When Karsten was a year old, his father migrated alone to Seattle and Americanized his name to Herman Andrew. One year after that, Herman sent for his wife, Ragna Koppen Solheim, and Karsten. Mother and child set sail for America, Karsten too young to remember the trip.

Karsten's early memory is of his mother in her coffin. She died June 27, 1914, after prematurely giving birth to his brother Ragnor, Americanized to Raymond. Karsten was not yet three years old. She had gotten pregnant right after arriving in Seattle but had also, perhaps aboard ship, contracted tuberculosis, a lung disease common at that time and a disease that was often fatal.

Ragna Solheim's death began an odyssey for Karsten, who was shuffled from family to family for the next several years of his life.

After the death of his mother, Karsten's father left for Alaska to seek work, leaving baby Ray to be cared for by a Norwegian family named Eriksen, who had been renting a room to the Solheims. Being prematurely born, Ray was tiny, weighing about two pounds at birth. The Eriksens fed him with an eyedropper and kept him warm by wrapping him in cotton wool and placing him in a shoe box on the warming oven above the stove. Amazingly, Ray would one day grow to be a very big man, much bigger than Karsten.

The Eriksens had four daughters of their own, the eldest a year older than Karsten's father. They knew they couldn't care for two boys, one of whom was an infant who needed constant care. So when Karsten's father moved to Alaska, he sent his older son to live with a German family named Himmelspech. About a year later, Karsten was sent to a Swedish family named Anderson.

Karsten barely spoke during the first several years of his life, and it's not hard to understand why. There he was, not quite three years old, having lost his mother and seeing his father leave him. He was in a strange country, where he began life in a Norwegian-speaking home, then moved to a home where German was spoken, then to a Swedish-speaking household. All the while, he was surrounded by Americans who spoke English. How confusing it must have been for him to move literally from one culture to another so many times during early childhood. He must have felt he had been abandoned.

Around the time Karsten turned six, he finally got some stability in his life when his father returned from Alaska and married the oldest of the Eriksen girls. They had no honeymoon. She simply moved into a new home with her husband and his two small boys. It was another change for Karsten, but it created a lasting, stable home life for him and his brother. In 1922, Karsten and Ray welcomed a baby sister, Elaine. Then, three years later, another baby was born to the Solheim family, a girl they named Marjorie.

A STABLE FAMILY—FINALLY

Although Karsten was finally in a stable home with his own father, he was barely communicative. By then, he had almost completely forgotten his native tongue, Norwegian. His stepmother once told Louise Solheim, Karsten's wife of more than sixty years, that he rarely said more than *smør og brød*—"bread and butter"—in Norwegian. What made things even more difficult for Karsten was that he was also small for his age, too small to start school. Although he probably would have learned English faster if he had been in school, his father and stepmother kept him out until he was seven years old. By then he had learned enough English to get by, yet he had to repeat first grade.

Karsten remained small for his age all the way through his high school years, not attaining his adult growth until after he was eighteen. Being smaller than most of his classmates, despite being two or three years older than most, Karsten became a battler. He may not have been as big as his classmates, but he wasn't going to allow himself to be pushed around. He stood up for himself, and he got into scraps with some of his classmates because of it. Ray, who would not get involved in Karsten's fights, often raced home to get his mother to come to break them up.

Karsten soon grew accustomed to his surroundings with his birth father and his wife, but the scars of his early family-to-family moves remained. He still feared that one day he would have to leave his family again—or that they would leave him. Ray had become sort of an adopted son of Herman Solheim's in-laws, so he was often invited back to the Eriksen home to spend the night. Karsten's father felt it only right to give Karsten the same privilege, so he delivered him to the Eriksens' one night. Family legend has it that Karsten, apparently believing he was being given away yet again, became hysterical. He cried so hard that his two teenage step-aunts had to walk him the twelve or thirteen blocks home in the middle of the night.

In addition to gaining some stability in his life, Karsten first learned of the Christian faith as a small boy. The newly formed Solheim family lived in the Ballard area of Seattle, a Scandinavian section of the city. Karsten's father, a Christian man himself, took his family to Bethel Temple, a Pentecostal mission in downtown Seattle, where, at the age of seven or eight, Karsten committed himself to the Christian faith. Many years later, he still vividly remembered being with his stepmother after hearing the sermon and "walking the aisle" to accept Christ. He remembered feeling at peace and good about what he'd done.

That night was the beginning of a long life of faith in God for Karsten Solheim, who operated his business and his personal life the best he knew how, using the Bible as a guide for all he did.

DEMONSTRATING EARLY GENIUS

Although Karsten didn't get his start in the golf equipment business till he was in his forties, long before that there were indications that this man would be something special in whatever field he entered. Those inklings of genius were evident from the time he started school. Looking back on that time in Karsten's life, it should be obvious to anyone who knew him that if it hadn't been golf equipment, it would have been something else.

By almost any standard, Karsten Solheim's start in school was a slow one. But once he got started, it seemed there was nothing he couldn't do, no idea he couldn't grasp, and no skill he couldn't master. The term "talented and gifted" as it is applied to schoolchildren was a gross understatement for a student such as Karsten. Math came easily to him, as did industrial arts. And in the subjects he didn't seem a "natural" at, he worked hard, achieving success through effort alone. He was always the kind of person who was driven to be the best he possibly could be in any area, and that included schoolwork.

He worked hard in school at first, but when he got into high school he became discouraged. He worked hard to get an A in a subject he didn't care for, and when he aced the test, the teacher couldn't believe it. He was accused of cheating. Dismayed, he decided to quit taking books home to study.

Karsten excelled most in math and woodworking. His woodwork was amazingly intricate, creative, and functional, particularly for a high school boy. In fact, he was so skilled with his hands that the two wood shop teachers at Ballard High School argued over who would have him in class. At one point they were hopelessly deadlocked and told him to just not take woodworking. Yet, when the principal needed a bookcase built, both teachers recommended Karsten for the job.

As he did with all his woodworking projects, he did a masterful job on the bookcase, which was still being used in the school fifty years later, with Karsten's signature on the back. More than sixty years after they were made, several of his projects still grace Louise's Phoenix home, as functional, sturdy, and visually appealing as they were when they were built. Visitors nearly always express astonishment that they were done by a high school boy more than a half century ago.

Karsten was also an excellent mechanic, and it seemed to come naturally to him. He had a seemingly innate ability to understand how things worked, a skill that would play a large part in his taking his place in the world of golf manufacturing. He had an uncanny knack for figuring out what was wrong with a machine, then fixing it on the spot. He could look at a machine, take it apart, analyze the problem, repair it, and reassemble it. He loved cars and engines and quickly became proficient at working on them, a skill that came in quite handy throughout his life.

As talented and intelligent as Karsten Solheim was as a youth, that would have meant little had he not also possessed that certain something within that made him the kind of man who persevered, who continued to work his hardest, even when things didn't go his way at first. He had that quality, and he had it in large quantities from the time he was a little boy.

LEARNING TO WORK

Nobody who knew Karsten Solheim, not even his wife and children, ever heard him complain about how hard he worked, even as a little boy in grade school. Karsten learned early the value of hard work, starting when he worked in his father's shoe-repair shop as a second grader. It seems cruel by today's standards to make a child that age work after school, but that was the way it was done in the Old Country, and that's how Karsten's father operated his shop.

Karsten started working in the shoe shop at a time when he was barely big enough to hold a broom in his hands. His father had him come right after school, which was only a few blocks from the shop, and work with him for the rest of the day. He swept the floor, washed the windows—whatever a boy that age was physically able to do. He even helped out at the counter, standing on a box to wait on customers because he was too short to see over the counter. As he got more and more accustomed to working, his father gradually taught him the shoe-repair trade. He always loved working with his hands and learning technical skills, so he took to shoe repair quickly at a very early age.

Karsten wasn't the kind of high school kid who let his time slip idly by. He was a busy high schooler who worked hard and had goals for his life. He wanted to become an engineer, and his goal was to graduate from the University of Washington. In addition to working to get good grades at Ballard High School, he rose early every morning to do a large paper route, saving the money he earned for college. After school, except during baseball season—he once lettered in high school baseball—it was straight to the shoe shop, where he worked until closing.

Karsten graduated from high school in 1931 and then enrolled at the University of Washington in Seattle, where he studied engineering. After just a year at college, however, the Great Depression made it impossible for him to continue school because he had run out of money. He dropped out of college, then moved to Port Townsend, Washington, where he took a job in the shoe-repair department at the back of Olberg's Department Store. His guaranteed wages were two dollars a day or half of what he took in.

Karsten had attended church his whole life, and he continued to attend in Port Townsend. He found he enjoyed services in the local Methodist church. There he met a farm family named Neville, which included four sons and parents, who made it a habit to invite people over for Sunday dinner. Karsten was one of those people, and he grew close to the family. He visited them often, even living with them for a time.

During that period, he continued to work with his

hands. One of the Neville boys, William, later remembered that Karsten made them a leather slingshot, the kind David might have used in Bible times. Karsten went with the boys to the bank overlooking Discovery Bay, and they enjoyed seeing who could sling a rock the farthest out into the Pacific. Forty-five years later, William Neville visited Karsten and gave him that same slingshot.

MEETING DESTINY—BACK HOME

Herman Solheim's shoe-repair business expanded until he was running two shops in Seattle. But a year after Karsten left for Port Townsend, his father suffered an illness that forced him to cut back on his hours of work and forced Karsten to return home to help him run the two shops. There was no question about it: Herman needed Karsten's help if the business was to survive. The shops stood six blocks apart on 24th Avenue NW. After his return to Seattle, Karsten ran one of them, and his father ran the other.

Karsten and his father operated the business with the utmost integrity, insisting—quietly—that those who came into the shop not disrespect their Christian beliefs. One of the Neville boys visited Karsten one day and recalls two women swearing as they conversed in the shop. Karsten said nothing. He merely found a small placard and quietly placed it on the counter in front of them. It read, "Thou shalt not take the name of the Lord thy God in vain." The women quickly fell silent.

Karsten Solheim was never one to be overly outspoken about anything, and that included his faith. Rather, he preferred to let his actions do the talking. His relationship with God soon took a prominent place in his life while he was still a young man. He was a behind-the-scenes servant at his church, Bethel Temple. He filled his big car with children he had invited to Sunday school. After the evening services, when he would drive his fellow youth group members

35

somewhere, he sometimes had to deliver a pair of shoes along the way. Often he drove groups to various other area churches where special services were held.

For eight years, Karsten would run the shoe-repair shop and center his leisure time on church. When he landed a huge army contract job, he worked mornings and most of the night filling the avalanche of orders on time.

It was an incredibly busy time in his life, and in the middle of that period Karsten met someone who, like himself, was a motherless child. As it turned out, that person would be the woman with whom he would share the rest of his life.

3

THE WOMAN OF HIS DREAMS

Louise

That's the man you're going to marry. It wasn't something she'd expected to hear ringing within her head. Nellie Louise Crozier was a seventeen-year-old schoolgirl when something—almost but not quite an audible voice, as she remembered it many years later—told her she was looking at the man who would be her husband. She wasn't looking for a husband at that time in her life. She was only a teenager, and she had so much to do before she settled down. First of all, she wanted to go to the University of Washington and graduate.

She didn't even know the man's name or anything else about him. She knew he was pleasing to the eye, that he had the most beautiful hair she could remember seeing on a man. There was something else about him, something she couldn't put her finger on. Yet that small voice within her told her that the handsome young man she saw in church was the man who should be her husband.

That handsome young man was Karsten Solheim.

Karsten sat with the Sunday school class he had been teaching. It was the church's annual Christmas program, and he was not unaware of Louise's presence or that she had noticed him. But he had no idea she looked at him with interest that night, no idea that she would become the most important person in his life for the next sixty-plus years, no idea that she was the ideal companion and partner for him in the journey that was ahead. And he also had no idea how similar her life as a child had been to his.

SIMILAR PATHS

Louise and Karsten met only in passing that winter day in 1935. Neither had any idea how similar their life journeys had been. Both had known happiness and joy in their young lives, but both had also known their share of sadness. Both had people who loved them very much, yet both had times in their lives when they felt uprooted or abandoned. Karsten had come from a background with a lot of hardship and sadness because of the loss of his mother. Louise was also a motherless child with much sadness in her past. In fact, the sadness that was a part of her family's life started many years before she was born.

Louise's grandmother on her father's side had been one of at least a dozen children. She was to endure more than her share of heartaches. Family lore says there wasn't much love or warmth in that crowded household. When she grew up, she married a Frenchman named Louis Solomon Crozier, and the couple had four children. Then the man abandoned her and the children, going to South America to make a fortune. He never returned.

The four Crozier children were parceled out to various family members, each to be raised by a different household. All four ran away from their various homes as youngsters.

One of the children, John Louis Crozier, left home when he was twelve years old, hopped a freight train, and set out for the Pacific Northwest. Big for his age and unusually studious for a virtually fatherless boy, he worked in a bakery and on farms, eventually putting himself through the University of Washington. When he finished his degree in education, he became a teacher. He later became a school superintendent but returned to teaching again when the administrative politics wore him down.

While a superintendent in northern Washington, John Crozier married a teacher named Nellie Nevada Oldham, and she soon became pregnant with their first and only child. At the end of the 1917–18 school year, John moved his young wife to Spokane. The baby was due in about a month, and he wanted her to have the best care possible.

Nellie Louise Crozier was born June 6, 1918, and the young couple called her Louise. That was when tragedy again struck the Crozier family. Her mother never got out of the hospital after Louise's birth. She contracted scarlet fever three days later and died within a month.

John Louis Crozier never remarried. Grief stricken at the loss of his wife, he moved to Seattle and tried to take care of baby Louise himself. He put her in various homes while he was working, but he never felt she was getting the care and attention she needed. John's sister, Louise Kinsler, who had settled in Austwell, Texas, on San Antonio Bay, offered to take in the baby and raise her with her four young daughters. John Louis refused, wanting to keep Louise near him in Washington.

Nearly a year after the death of his wife, John finally found a couple who seemed to take good care of his daughter. They soon fell in love with her, though, and told him they couldn't keep on taking care of her unless they could adopt her and become her legal parents. To John that was out of the question. He needed help to care for his daughter, but he wasn't about to give her away. He contacted his sister and took her up on her offer to care for Louise.

Aunt Louise had married well. Her husband, John Kinsler, was a farmer with thousands of Texas acres. There was no question her aunt and uncle would be more than able financially to take care of the baby. Aunt Louise and her oldest daughter, Katharine, came for Louise in Seattle and took her to Texas before she was a year old. Two years younger than the Kinslers' youngest daughter, Louise became the baby of five girls. She would stay there nine years and come to know her aunt and uncle as Mother and Daddy. Her cousins became her sisters. And because one of the other girls was already named Louise, the family called the new baby Nellie from the time she arrived.

A LOVING FAMILY

Uncle John Kinsler was a warm and affectionate father figure. Little Nellie loved him dearly. Moving to Texas into a big, loving family was the best thing that could have happened to her. The expansive acreage, the various pets, the proximity to San Antonio Bay, where she could go fishing, crabbing, and walk the shore—everything contributed to a happy childhood.

There was, however, a busybody who worked at the drugstore in town. When Nellie was about three years old, this woman told her that John and Louise Kinsler were not really her parents but rather her aunt and uncle, and the four girls she thought were her sisters were actually her cousins. Today Louise Solheim doesn't remember that conversation, but her aunt once told her how upset everyone was over it. All Louise recalls is that she knew she had a different father from the rest of the girls, one she called Daddy Louis. And she knew her real mother had died.

As she remembers, Daddy Louis was able to visit her only twice in nine years before coming one final time to take her back to Washington. He wrote her regularly, though, and sent her gifts. She remembers getting at least one five-dollar gold piece and another time some beautiful clothes that she wore to Sunday school. He visited her for the first time when she was about six. It was novel to have her own father there, but it also upset her. She loved her "own" family and happily settled back into the routine when he left.

Nellie, as they called her, was a precocious child. Strangely, she was closest to her eldest cousin, Katharine, who was more than ten years older than she. Katharine became like a little mother to Nellie, teaching her to read even before she started school. In fact, Katharine says Nellie read as early as age three and then began to read everything in sight.

Apparently this news did not sit well with her educator father, who wrote that he felt the older girls' books were not appropriate for a preschooler. He was especially displeased a few years later when he discovered that she was already reading Zane Grey books. Nellie was unaware of her father's letters until later, and she still believes that reading those "older" books was a great start for her education. She would skip the first grade, something that also upset her birth father. Katharine herself graduated from high school at fifteen, got her master's in dietetics from the University of Chicago at twenty, and went on to teach at Michigan State University. Today Louise Solheim says that Katharine was her role model.

GETTING TO KNOW GOD IN TEXAS

Some of the earliest "readers" Nellie enjoyed were overtly religious. One was about a lead character named Elsie Dinsmore, who was "saved." Nellie was fascinated by this, partly because Elsie's mother had also died and Elsie was living with cousins. She felt a kinship with the Elsie character, and she also felt a need to be "saved," just as Elsie had been. Nellie wasn't exactly sure what being saved meant, but with the simple, uncluttered faith of a small child, she prayed one day while practicing the piano. She bowed her head and said, "Jesus, I want to be saved."

Although Nellie may not have totally understood what it meant to be "saved," she enjoyed Sunday school and church. Which denomination the church happened to be each week depended on which circuit-riding preacher was in town. Her Sunday school teacher impressed upon her that everything in the Bible was true, and she never doubted that the rest of her life. Her love for the Bible started when she was a child and hasn't waned to this day.

Nellie loved all the old hymns they sang in church. Though she recalls being told she was unable to carry a tune as a child, at home she often took a hymnbook and sat up on a cistern, where she sang her favorites at the top of her lungs.

These were the outward manifestations of a love for God, for His Word, and for His people that Louise would carry with her throughout her life. God was important to her, and she would take her relationship with Him away from the only home she could remember, when she would one day be reunited with her birth father and moved to Seattle.

GOING HOME

Nellie thrived and was a happy girl growing up with her aunt and uncle and cousins. But the time came when she would be permanently reunited with her father. It was a traumatic time for her, and it started, as she remembers now, with a little conflict in her Texas home.

The Kinslers had a lot of minority workers on the farm and in the house, and Nellie learned early what her elders considered appropriate distance from the ones they referred to as "darkies." One day one of the black girls was doing the dishes, and Nellie was chatting with her. Without a second thought, Nellie began drying the dishes as she made conversation with the girl. Her aunt noticed and called her out of the room. "Don't ever do that again," she said. "That's their job." Nellie obeyed, but to her it didn't seem right. What was wrong with helping someone with her work while you were talking?

For the most part, the five girls did few chores. There was enough paid help that Nellie and her cousins were free to play, read, or explore. But when she was about eight, Uncle John became frustrated because it seemed to him the girls were "growing up not knowing how to do anything." Nellie was assigned the job of scrubbing the upstairs bathtub every day, and, unbeknownst to her, the rest of the girls were also assigned daily chores. She didn't know everyone else had chores, too, and after having been told not to do the black girls' work, she began to feel that she was being treated poorly.

Nellie wrote her father and complained that her aunt and uncle were being mean to her. "Come and get me," she wrote.

The following summer, when she was nine, her father came to visit again, this time for a month. By then the chore crisis had long blown over, and Nellie believed she was as content as a child could be. But the visit from her father upset her to the point where she was no longer the happy-go-lucky, singing girl her family had come to know. Her aunt remembered that Nellie would sing when she came to the door with her hands full, "Open the door for the children." She never did that while her real father was there, clearly worried what his presence would mean to her future. The singing stopped with her father's arrival.

Early on in his visit, John Crozier took her for a walk in the pasture. "I received your letter," he said. It all came back to Nellie, and she panicked. Maybe he had come to rescue her, but now she didn't want to be rescued at all! She told her father she didn't know anything about the letter.

"I didn't write you a letter," she said, but he pressed her, knowing beyond a doubt all the time that she had, in fact, written, asking him to come for her.

"Oh, you didn't? Well, it sure looked like your handwriting."

Nellie told him that a neighbor girl her age had handwriting that looked just like hers. "She must have written it."

But he said, "Why would she write to me and pretend to be you, complaining about being mistreated?"

"I don't know, but it wasn't me, so it must have been her!"

Her father let the matter drop, but she knew she had not convinced him. She was miserable over what was happening. The guilt of lying to her father and her anxiety over perhaps having to leave the only home she had ever known made her sick to her stomach. She retreated to her bedroom, claiming illness. It seemed that her whole world was collapsing around her and that there was nothing she could do about it.

After a month of the turmoil, Nellie awoke relieved. It was the day her father was to leave. She loved her father, but she didn't want to leave her aunt and uncle's home. While saying good-bye to her, however, he told her that the following year he would come for her and she would be coming home to Washington to live with him. "I will come for you next summer, so be prepared," he said.

It had been John Crozier's intent from the beginning to bring his daughter back to Washington to live with him, as soon as he was able to care for her.

Nellie still didn't like the idea of leaving Texas, but a year seemed a long time, and she accepted her fate. She was so relieved when her father left that her stomachache went away and she became bubbly and began singing again. She gradually even began to accept the fact that she would be moving away to live with him. Over the next year she got used to the idea that her long stay in Texas would soon be over.

A couple of months after Nellie's tenth birthday, in the summer of 1928, John Louis Crozier was true to his word. He came for her.

The day before she was to leave with him on the train, Daddy Kinsler woke her early. She had been so close to him, and she thought of him as her father. She loved his warmth and tender touch. That day, he did a wonderful thing for the little girl. He took her in his truck to all the properties he owned and farmed so that she could say good-bye to all the foremen and the workers. She simply loved having her uncle's full attention for the whole day. It was a wonderful day for her, but it was also a sad one, for it was the day that her uncle—this warm, sweet, wonderful man who had been the father figure in her life—said his good-bye to her.

When the rest of the family saw her and her father off at the train the next day, her Uncle John was not there. They had already said their good-byes, and apparently a final farewell would have been too much for Uncle John to bear. She and Uncle John had grown to love one another deeply, and parting was hard for them both. Her uncle just couldn't bring himself to see her off at the train station. Nellie found out later from her youngest cousin that Uncle John had gone to the bay and walked up and down the shoreline all day, grieving because little Nellie was leaving for good.

Nellie's aunt, though she had never been terribly affectionate, spoke to Nellie privately on the train platform. "It will be different up in Washington, but he'll take good care of you. He loves you," she said It was an emotional moment for Nellie, but she held her own. Tears were in her eyes, but she held her head high so they wouldn't roll down her cheeks and people would see that she was crying. She boarded the train with her father and left the only family she had ever known.

It was time for her to start a new life with her natural father, John Crozier.

ADJUSTING TO HOME

The train ride back to Washington took several weeks, because Nellie's father first took her to Indiana to meet her mother's parents. It was the only time she ever saw her maternal grandparents. It was on to St. Louis to see her mother's brother and his family, then to Kansas where her father was raised. She had been there nearly every summer because her aunt had taken her and her four cousins to visit.

Nellie loved waking up in the sleeping berth in the middle of the night and seeing the towns and depots roll by, wondering about the people on the platform and on the train. She also loved eating in the dining car. She has become a world traveler and believes her love of travel began back then.

When Nellie and her father finally reached Washington, she was in for a big adjustment. First, he called her Louise, and she resisted being called Louise. *He's trying to change everything,* she thought. She said she preferred Nellie. She eventually decided she wanted to be called Louise and came to prefer it, but she would not officially change her name until she graduated from high school.

John Crozier and his daughter settled in Renton, a suburb of Seattle, which was just about as far from Texas culturally as it was in miles. Her father taught science and business in the junior and senior high school, where she would attend. She felt awkward that her father was a teacher in her school. It seemed strange to have to call him Mr. Crozier, but kids laughed when she called him Daddy. However, she adjusted to that and soon began excelling in school.

One other adjustment for Louise was that of the difference in cultures between Texas and the Pacific Northwest. Having skipped a grade, she was already entering sixth grade and, fortunately, was tall for her age. That helped her fit in, once the kids tired of making fun of her Texan accent and her yes sirs and no ma'ams. The school was much bigger than she was used to. Rather than having two classes in the same room, each class had its own homeroom. They then went to other teachers' rooms for different subjects.

With her natural mother long since passed away, theirs was a lonely household, just Louise and her father. She missed having a mother figure in her life, even if her aunt hadn't been the most affectionate or demonstrative woman around. She missed Texas and the family she had known practically all her life. Eventually, though, she decided to accept the change, realizing that she belonged with her birth father.

It took Louise time to adjust to the differences between her birth father and her uncle. John Crozier had built a wall around his emotions after the death of his wife, and he was not the affectionate and loving man that her uncle was. He was difficult to get to know, but she found him patient and kind and encouraging. He taught her to shop, to clean, to cook, to dress a chicken. He taught her every manner of household chore, and it wasn't long before Louise realized that whatever she was learning would soon become her job.

John Crozier made sure that she had as balanced a life as could be expected under the circumstances. In addition to the household duties he taught her, he also saw to it that she learned to swim, play the piano, and sing. She also took lessons in public speaking.

While John Crozier was patient with Louise in almost every area, the one area in which her father was short with her was when she mentioned her family in Texas. Perhaps from insecurity or jealousy, he seemed to find it necessary to criticize them whenever she talked about them, so she learned not to bring up that subject.

At first the Kinslers wrote her often, but for some reason—perhaps her disastrous letter to her father had scared her away from letter writing—Louise did not write back, and their letters became more infrequent. Whenever she got a letter from her uncle, she would not open it until she could be alone, because she would begin crying even before she opened it.

MAKING A COMMITMENT TO GOD

When Louise first came back to Washington with her father, they lived with a family in town, but then they moved to his "farm." Actually, calling it a farm was a bit of a stretch. It wasn't more than two acres, and it was located in an area that Louise recalls seeming more like a retirement community, because all the neighbors were elderly people.

Among those neighbors, though, was a family who eventually helped guide Louise along the path that solidified her relationship with God.

Across the way from the Crozier farm lived a couple named LaDuke. The woman, a widow who had remarried, had a son who brought his wife and two young daughters to visit from California. One of the girls, Margie Cross, was only a couple of years younger than Louise. They became fast friends, and, in fact, they remain so to this day.

Margie and her family attended church every Sunday when visiting her grandmother. She often came back from the services and repeated the sermons to Louise, as well as she could remember them. Louise enjoyed hearing about Margie's church. Eventually the family invited her to go with them, and again she felt at home. When Margie and her family were not visiting, Louise would frequently visit the LaDuke family and talk about the things of the Bible.

Margie was the first person Louise would hear use the term "born again" for the spiritual conversion she was convinced Louise needed. Louise had wanted to be "saved" when she was a little girl in Texas, and when Margie told her that the Bible said she needed to be born again, Louise wanted to know all about it. If there was one thing she believed, it was that every word of the Bible was true.

One day, while at church with Margie's family, Louise walked forward to the altar after the service and prayed to receive Christ into her life. Though her father did not encourage her in her spiritual life, and she rarely went to church unless Margie's family was visiting, Louise believes she felt the hand of God on her life from an early age.

EXCELLING IN SCHOOL

Louise always loved school and excelled in it, particularly in math and science. She had started reading at a very young age, and her love for the written word has continued all her life. She also enjoyed sports such as softball and volleyball, and some sort of extracurricular activity was required by the Torch Society (honor society). Her father had chosen all her subjects to ensure she would be prepared for college. All subjects, that is, except one.

When Louise became a senior, her father told her to sign up for zoology, because he thought it would fit in well with her academic background in math and science. She wanted to take journalism, but the school had dropped it during the Depression-induced budget cuts. The principal called Louise in and told her they were reestablishing the journalism class and that her English teachers had recommended her for it. That appealed to Louise, so she went home and told her father.

"What would you have to drop?" he asked.

"Zoology."

"No, you can't do that. With all your math and science background, zoology is just what you need now."

When the school principal called Louise back in for her decision, she felt pleased that she was so eagerly wanted. And to her this was an adult decision, one she had to make despite the consequences. She dropped zoology and signed up for journalism without telling her father.

In spite of making all A's except for a B in geometry that term, Louise did not volunteer to show her father her report card as usual. She didn't want him to know she had defied him and dropped zoology. As a teacher, though, he knew full well when her report card had come out. "Let me see it," he said.

Mr. Crozier studied the report card and noticed there was no grade for zoology. "Where's your zoology grade?" he asked his daughter.

"I dropped it to take journalism," she said, wondering what his response would be.

Her father said nothing. He just put the report card on the table and walked away. That was one of the few times she remembers disobeying her dad. She has always been a people pleaser, and she had been taught well, in Texas and in Washington, to obey her elders. Louise felt bad that she had disappointed her father, yet she was also glad she had taken the journalism course. In her junior and senior years, she had won the school's short story contest and for years has kept up with her many friends and relatives with regular journal-type letters.

A FORK IN THE ROAD

Renton High School had an excellent boys' basketball team. In fact, the team was so good that it won the state championship Louise's senior year, and she dated one of the players for two years. Her mind, however, was mostly on her studies. She dreamed of attending the University of Washington as her father had. She would wind up fifth of 120 students in the 1935 class of Renton High School. She graduated just before her seventeenth birthday, having excelled in her university entrance exams. A student at UW told her she had scored the highest among women applicants.

Before she could set foot in a University of Washington classroom, however, she faced the biggest disappointment of her life since having to return to Seattle from Texas. A few days after her high school graduation, while she was planning a summer partly of freedom and partly of work to earn money for college, her father made an announcement. He had decided she was too young for the University of Washington.

He wanted her to go to business college first, where, he said, she would learn skills that would help her later at the university. Louise was deeply disappointed. She didn't want to go to business school. But her father contacted a representative of the school, and he visited their home. Louise began to suspect that the reason had as much to do with the shortage of money during the Depression as with her age. Finally, although she didn't want to forgo attending UW, she said, "If that's what you want me to do, Daddy, I will."

She did, too. The summer following her senior year passed quickly, and during her first year out of high school, Louise Crozier attended Wilson Modern Business College. She enrolled under the name of Louise and never answered to Nellie again.

Although she was disappointed that she wasn't attending the University of Washington, Louise would soon live through a chain of events—one of the first being enrolling at business school—that would bring her in contact with Karsten Solheim, the man she saw one Sunday in a church service when she heard something tell her that he would one day be her husband.

4

THE
MEETING

Love at First Sight?

Louise Crozier was displeased that her father wouldn't allow her to enroll at the University of Washington, but she obeyed his wishes. Immediately she moved from Renton to Seattle and enrolled at Wilson Modern Business College, where she studied, still hoping one day to enroll at UW.

Even if it wasn't what she wanted to be doing at that time, she made the best of her situation. For her board and room she worked for a plumber's family on Capital Hill, not far from the school. The home she worked at was also close to Bethel Temple, a church her friend Margie Cross had told her about. It had a huge young people's group that met on Saturday nights and was within walking distance of where she lived.

Louise wanted to check out the young people's group. When a young man at the business college asked her for a date, she agreed to go with him one October evening if he would take her to Bethel Temple on Saturday night.

What Louise thought was to be a youth meeting turned out also to be one where people talked about their personal spiritual journeys. When, as part of her "testimony," a black woman sang a long, enthusiastic version of "This World Is Not My Home," the singer danced up and down the aisles from front to back, singing all the verses of the song. Louise had never seen anything like that in church and was deeply moved. Her date thought the whole thing was funny. But it didn't seem right to Louise that this young man would laugh at the woman. It seemed rude, and it seemed inappropriate at church.

Although Louise didn't date the young man again, she did return to Bethel Temple by herself the next night for the Sunday evening service. Years later, she couldn't remember much about the program or the sermon, but she remembers well her sense of need to make a commitment to God. She had been living what she considered an inconsistent Christian life. Her church attendance was spotty when Margie Cross was not visiting and being a good influence and going to church with her. Louise had made a statement of her faith and had been baptized several years before that, but she knew her commitment to God wasn't what it needed to be.

Now it was time for her to make a decision. She knew she had to choose sides. She knew she had to make some changes in her life. She had to decide where her loyalty was. To herself? To the world? To her education? Or to Jesus Christ?

At the end of the meeting, Louise, by now in tears, hurried to the altar and prayed, committing her life to God. She told Him she was finally ready to give Him her all. A young couple, Hilding and Gertrude Halvarson, took her home. They would be lifelong friends.

After that night, she felt new. She knew she had changed something inside her. She found she had a new enthusiasm for life, for her work, for her studies, but especially for the things of God. She read her Bible with deeper understanding, went to Bethel Temple regularly, and felt her very desires had changed.

Louise also felt the need to make things right with her aunt and uncle in Texas and her father. She remembered the letter she had written to her father and then denied writing. She wrote to him and to her aunt and uncle, admitting for the first time that she had written that fateful letter nearly nine years earlier and apologizing for any hurt she had caused. Her aunt answered immediately with a very warm letter, saying there was nothing to forgive. They realized Louise had been just a child, she said, and she was happy that Louise was happy. Still, writing to them was something Louise felt she needed to do, and doing it got rid of the guilt of having hurt the ones she loved so much.

Louise was in church whenever she had free time—at the worship services, at Sunday school, and at youth meetings. One of the girls in the youth group approached her one day. She told Louise that she herself had attended church for two years before she made any friends and that she didn't want that to happen to anyone else who came. "So, welcome to Bethel Temple," she said, smiling.

With this attentive young woman taking Louise under her wing, she quickly made friends at the church. Bethel Temple was growing rapidly. There were perhaps a thousand members at the time, including about one hundred in the youth group. The church also supported many missionaries on foreign fields. Louise always looked forward to church and youth group, and by December of that year (1935) she had begun helping out with various projects. She was asked to assist with the Sunday school Christmas program, which was held December 22.

That turned out to be one of the most important days of her life.

THE MEETING

Karsten Solheim was twenty-four years old, and he was active in his church, Bethel Temple in Seattle. As a young man, he was very serious about his faith and about serving God in any way he could. Among other activities, he helped with the young people in the church and was a Sunday school teacher for junior-high-aged kids. The day of the Christmas program, Karsten sat with a group of his students in the church's choir loft.

Louise Crozier had been asked to help direct children to their seats, and by the time she had finished that task, the program had already begun. Feeling a little self-conscious, she didn't want to walk across the platform to find a seat in the crowded auditorium. Instead, she made her way to the choir loft, where she found the last available seat in the top row.

Once settled, she glanced down the row at several ten-to twelve-year-old boys. With them was a nice-looking young man. Years later, she still remembered how taken she was by him and how beautiful and curly his hair was.

Something about him struck a chord inside her. It was as if God Himself was telling her that she would marry that man—and sooner than she had planned marriage. That didn't make a lot of sense to her. She was only seventeen years old, and she had so much to do before she could get married and start a family. Still, she had a hard time not looking at him, especially after hearing that "voice" saying, *That's the man you are going to marry.* She had to find out who he was.

When the program was over, Louise asked her friend about the young man down the row. She didn't get a lot of information, just his name. Even then, it was just his first name, which she didn't hear right.

"Oh, that's Karsten," she said, but Louise heard "Carson."

"Carson?" she said. "What's his first name?"

"I don't know. He's just Karsten."

Louise still heard "Carson."

And suddenly, here he came. He walked up to Louise and her friend, smiled warmly at them, and said hello. Before they could even be introduced, he said, "Do you like fudge?"

"Well, sure," Louise said.

"I'll go get some," Karsten said and went off to get some of the candy that he'd brought to give to the custodian, pianist, and others who had taken part in the program.

Louise was impressed with the soft-spoken, pleasant man she thought was named Carson. She didn't know where he was going to get the fudge, but she had the impression he would be right back. He didn't return right away, though, and she waited about ten minutes before heading home. She figured he'd gotten interrupted on his way to get the fudge and couldn't make it back. It wasn't long, though, before Karsten and Louise would meet again.

The next night, both had to be back at church to rehearse for Tuesday's Christmas Eve pageant. She was playing the innkeeper's wife and Karsten a shepherd. With such small roles, they found themselves waiting for long stretches, and they had time to talk. Karsten got the chance to ask Louise what had happened the day before, why she hadn't waited.

"I'm Karsten," he said, smiling. "Karsten Solheim." He explained that he had brought the homemade fudge as gifts for several people and left it in an office. But when he went to get it, the office was locked, and he had to find a janitor to let him in. "By the time I got back, you were gone. I understood."

What a wonderful guy, Louise thought.

He had a soft, mellow voice and spoke deliberately, and he told her a good bit of his personal history right away. He also asked Louise a lot of questions about herself. He told her that he had been born in Norway but moved to the United States as a small boy. He told her he was a shoemaker who ran a shop for his father. He also told her he had been engaged twice before, adding with a smile, "Maybe the Lord saved the best for the last."

The look on his face left no doubt what he was talking about, and it took Louise by surprise. *Wait a minute!* she thought. *This is going a little too fast.* Still, there was something about this man that put her at ease.

And then, with a twinkle in his eye, Karsten said, "You heard the sermon last night, right?"

Indeed she had. The guest speaker had been an evangelist by the name of William Booth-Clibborn, and he spoke on man, woman, and marriage. Louise had enjoyed the sermon, but one thing stood out that night. Booth-Clibborn said the ideal age for marriage was when a man was twenty-five and a woman was eighteen—a seven-year difference.

Louise told Karsten she remembered what had been said.

"How old are you?" he asked her.

"Seventeen. How old are you?"

"Twenty-four."

The implication was not lost on either of them. They had met the day before and were talking for the first time now, but within a year they would each be the perfect age for marriage, according to William Booth-Clibborn. It was that same seven-year difference.

She laughed. He laughed. And they kept chatting.

The Christmas pageant was held the next night, and again they spoke briefly. Louise reminded herself that she was not looking for a husband. She was not even looking for a boyfriend.

Louise had lost interest in business school, where she had excelled in some things and not in others, particularly shorthand. She had dropped out and was now living with her father. She didn't know what she wanted to be. She had thought of being a dietitian, like her cousin Katharine, but she felt no clear direction. What she did know was that she wanted to keep going the twenty-five miles from Renton to Bethel Temple to attend her church and, especially, so that she could see Karsten Solheim.

The next Sunday, Louise had arranged to spend the night with a girlfriend in Seattle. But when Karsten saw her, he said he had brought his car and he could drive her home to Renton if she wished. Of course she wished. If it would give her more time to talk to him, she would most certainly let him drive her home.

Louise quickly ran to her girlfriend and told her the news. The friend understood completely, and Louise enjoyed the long drive and even longer conversation with Karsten.

He was such a serious young man and a deep thinker. He also seemed very sincere to her. There was no posturing. There were no games. He told her up front that he had been engaged twice before, but that he had never really asked either girl to marry him. Apparently these were casual relationships that had been encouraged by peers, and he felt he had little control of them until the engagements broke. He told her he wouldn't date just for fun, that he wouldn't hold a girl's hand unless he was in love with her, and that he wouldn't kiss her unless they were engaged.

To a teenage girl this talk was exhilarating. She wasn't sure what she thought of this new friend, but she certainly liked his ideas and his convictions. She had never had this kind of conversation with a man, and she enjoyed it. It made her want to get to know him better. When they finally arrived at her home, all the lights were off. Louise's father had assumed, of course, that she was staying in Seattle with her girlfriend, so he was in bed asleep, lights off, doors locked. Karsten had to help Louise climb through her bedroom window, and both thought they had done it silently.

They were wrong.

SHOTGUN IN THE WINDOW

As Karsten drove away, John Louis Crozier was grabbing his shotgun and following the sounds of what he thought was a prowler in his daughter's bedroom. He went outside and walked around the house to Louise's window, ready at the very least to throw a scare into the supposed intruder.

As Louise knelt by her bed to pray, she heard noises at the window and froze. The window slowly rose, and the curtains parted to reveal the barrel of a shotgun. She didn't move or breathe until she saw her father's silhouette in the window.

"Oh, Daddy! It's just me!" she cried out. "The door was locked. I should have knocked."

Of course, John Crozier wanted to know why she was home and not with her girlfriend in town. She told him briefly about the young man who had driven her home. But her father didn't want to hear about her being out with a boy, and he told her she was far too young to be thinking about boys.

"He's no boy, Daddy," Louise protested. "He's twenty-four years old."

That made the situation even worse in her father's eyes. "Even more reason for you not to be thinking about him," he said.

But Louise could think of little else but Karsten. She was enamored of this young man, and she had a lot of reasons. He was kind. He was fun loving, yet soft-spoken almost to the point of shyness. He was a behind-the-scenes person, but seemingly known and admired and respected by most everyone. He was very active in the church—driving kids everywhere, going to special meetings, volunteering for various ministries. He taught one Sunday school class at Bethel Temple and a second class at another church.

His churchgoing was not just a social or public thing, either. He had a personal faith. His first letter to her contained Proverbs 3:5–6, which would become their life verses: "Trust in the Lord with all thine heart; and lean not unto thine own understanding. In all thy ways acknowledge him, and he shall direct thy paths."

Louise loved his love of Scripture, his handsome face, his curly hair. And it was clear that he was industrious, hardworking. Quiet as he was in public, in private he was a talker. He had convictions, ideas, plans. That attracted her to him all the more. He was curious about everything. Life and people fascinated him.

Professionally, Karsten's life was fixing shoes, but in his private life he was about ministering to others. He visited jails, old folks' homes, taught Sunday school, and did whatever he could to make sure others had a chance to get to church and hear the gospel. Louise knew about those things from others, mostly, because Karsten didn't talk about such activities much, if at all. He told her that he didn't want people to know what he was doing. As far as he was concerned, that was between him and the Lord.

She had known Karsten eight days, from one Sunday to the next, and yet she felt she had known him all her life. He had been so forthcoming, so serious, that it almost alarmed her. But she found his honesty refreshing. He knew who he was, what he wanted, where he was going. Yet he didn't talk as much about himself as his projects. She learned about him through what he said about the things he was doing.

Karsten did express definite ideas about a potential wife, and the implication was that if Louise agreed to keep seeing him, she might as well know what those ideas were.

She liked what she had heard so far, but she had come a long way from not looking for a husband to wondering how she matched Karsten Solheim's dreams and wishes. All in a space of eight days!

As for Karsten, he had been smitten with this pretty young woman. She dominated his thoughts that week. He liked everything he had seen in her during that short time. She was bright and smart and humble, but most of all, she was spiritual. There was no question in his mind that her conversion experience had been real, and he loved hearing of her recent rededication experience, because it showed in her life.

Karsten Solheim knew at that time that Louise was the woman he wanted to spend his life with. And to his way of thinking, there was no point in waiting to do something about that. He was going to propose. And he was going to do it sooner rather than later.

5

A HOPE DEFERRED, A DESIRE REALIZED

Getting Engaged and Married—Quickly

Karsten Solheim never was one to dillydally when it came to getting what he wanted, and his proposal to Louise Crozier was certainly no exception. In a time when single people are told to date as long as they can in order to get to know someone, it seems almost unbelievable that Karsten and Louise Solheim got engaged less than two weeks after they met.

In the week that followed their first meeting, Karsten was certain that Louise was the woman he wanted to marry. She was everything he was looking for and more. Although he had just met her, he was in love and wanted to make her his bride as soon as possible.

A scant ten days from their first meeting, Karsten and Louise met at the church's watch night service on New

Year's Eve, and then he took her out to a special spot. Louise began to wonder what was on his mind. She wondered if it was possible he planned to ask her to marry him that very night. Could he possibly be thinking seriously about asking her to marry him, when they had known one another only a week and a half? One thing was sure in her mind, whether it was tonight or some distant day in the future, Karsten would have to verbally propose to her. And she would not tell him of the voice that spoke when she first saw him.

Karsten began talking of the future, about the possibility of God's call on his life.

Louise felt overwhelmed by what she was hearing, and she desperately wanted to know what to do if he popped the question. She prayed silently, at the same time listening to this man with whom she had already fallen in love. She knew it wasn't conventional wisdom—even back then—for people who had just met to get married, but she still wondered. Could this possibly be God's will? Had God, when she least expected it and when she wasn't looking for it at all and when she had so much to do with her life, brought her husband into her world? Her thoughts swirled around her, and she still didn't know what she would say if Karsten asked her to marry him.

"I'm a cobbler now," he said, "but there was a time when I thought God might call me into the ministry. Maybe as a pastor. Maybe even as a missionary." She could tell by his tone that he had something very, very serious to talk to her about, and finally it came out. "What I need to know is, if God called me, would you go with me?"

Louise still wasn't sure how to respond. Deep in her heart she wanted to say yes. She wanted this to happen. Though she'd known this man less than two weeks, she knew she wanted to marry him. She knew that the small voice she'd heard inside when she first saw him was speaking again, the voice that had told her he was the one she would spend her life with. But who would understand? Who would believe they could have known each other long enough to make such a decision? *She* didn't even believe that!

"I'm not a good housekeeper," she blurted.

Karsten, though, was undaunted. Quickly and smoothly, he let her know that her lack of domestic skills was not going to dissuade him. He wanted her to be his wife, not his maid.

"I don't want a housekeeper," he said. "I want a wife," not saying it specifically but leaving no doubt in Louise's mind that he wanted *her* to be his wife.

So there it was. He couldn't have been more specific. There was now no doubt in her mind that this was a proposal of marriage. He wanted her to be his wife, and he wanted an answer that night.

She looked away, unable to speak. She knew that anything but a yes would be a no to Karsten. If she wanted to wait, to think, to pray more, to take some time—all that might seem like rejection to him. She didn't want to lose him, and yet she wouldn't say yes too early just to keep him. If he loved her and cared for her and wanted her to be his wife, he would understand her misgivings and not pressure her.

Yet the question hung in the air. She had to give him an answer that night.

Suddenly Louise felt a sense of peace. She *knew* this was right, that it was good, that it was of God. It was hardly a matter of whether she could do better. If she waited years and searched the world over, she was convinced she would not find a more perfect husband. Something inside her had told her that Karsten was the one. She stalled for time. "I believe it is the Lord's will," she said.

Karsten was astonished. "I wouldn't have asked you if I hadn't felt that!" he said.

Now she felt free to answer. She answered him the way he hoped she would, but with one condition.

"Yes, Karsten," she said. "I'll be your wife. You'll have to ask my father, of course, but we should wait a couple of weeks for that."

Karsten Solheim did as his prospective bride asked: He waited a while before asking John Crozier for his daughter's hand in marriage.

SEEKING PERMISSION

Two weeks after Karsten Solheim proposed to Louise, she waited in another room at her home while Karsten talked with her father. She couldn't wait to hear the answer, although she wondered how Karsten was going to sell her father on the idea of his seventeen-year-old daughter getting married.

Karsten returned to her, downcast. It was a good-news/bad-news announcement he had to make to her, and the bad news was what she feared. John Crozier wouldn't approve of their getting married at her age. "He says you're too young," Karsten said. "He told me that if and when you married, he would want you to marry someone like me. But he said you are too young and should not marry yet." He looked at her expectantly. He could not—would not—pressure her to go against an influence as powerful as her father.

Louise thought of the high school decision she had made, choosing journalism over zoology. She had felt bad about going against her father's will, but if that had been an adult decision worth making independently, what was this? She decided at that moment that she and Karsten would get married, with or without her father's blessing.

"I'll be eighteen on June sixth," she said. "And then I won't need his permission."

Karsten urged that they hang onto Proverbs 13:12:

"Hope deferred maketh the heart sick: but when the desire cometh, it is a tree of life." He put three Scripture verses in his first letter to her. The first one was Proverbs 3:5–6, "Trust in the Lord with all thine heart; and lean not unto thine own understanding. In all thy ways acknowledge him, and he shall direct thy paths." The second was Proverbs 18:22: "Whoso findeth a wife findeth a good thing, and obtaineth favour of the Lord." The last one was Proverbs 13:12, which meant to Karsten that he and Louise couldn't get married right away, because of her father's objections. At least not till Louise's eighteenth birthday.

They set their wedding day for June 20, 1936. Louise's father was not pleased at that announcement. He refused to give his blessing or have anything to do with the planning, but he did not completely turn his back on his daughter and future son-in-law. "I'll not attend," he told her. "But I will give you one hundred dollars and provide the meat for the wedding supper." From his chicken house, Mr. Crozier would select two prize hens.

GETTING TO KNOW KARSTEN

The wedding supper was to be held at Karsten's parents' house. Louise had met them only after she and Karsten were engaged.

Mrs. Solheim told Louise there were things she needed to know about Karsten before they got married. She told her that he had been a strange child to raise, that he'd had a tough start to his life, that he'd fought a lot as a child, had been small for his age, and often dawdled. When she sent him to the store for something, he'd get distracted and wind up playing or watching some construction and not come back for hours.

On Karsten's part, he'd never had a bad thing to say about his father and stepmother. In his mind, their relationship with him was fine. Of course, he had gotten a lot of spankings—about one every day from his father—but he must have deserved them.

Louise stared at her future mother-in-law, wondering if she was serious. She wondered if Karsten's stepmother really understood him. The listed offenses made the young Karsten Solheim sound to Louise like a typical little boy. Mrs. Solheim, however, concluded that he was, on the whole, not really dependable, even now that he was a full-grown man.

How could this be? Louise wondered. He was a serious young man, and he had plans and goals. He ran one of his father's shoe-repair shops. He was active in church and volunteered for many duties. To her, he was ideal husband material. She said, "I think he's a wonderful man."

"Oh yes," Mrs. Solheim said quickly. "He's a very nice boy, but—"

And there she fell silent.

Louise was not dissuaded. Rather, she was all the more convinced that Karsten had been misunderstood. She understood him well. He was deep, he was thoughtful, and he would make a perfect husband. She was as sure as ever that she would go through with marrying this man.

A NEW LIFE TOGETHER

Karsten and Louise had been thinking of a church wedding, but Mrs. Solheim quickly quashed that hope. She made clear that it would be impossible to have a church wedding on Mr. Crozier's $100. So on June 20, 1936, shortly after Louise's eighteenth birthday, Karsten and Louise were married in the home of their pastor, the Reverend William Offiler. Karsten's brother, Ray, and Louise's best friend, Florence Johnson, were attendants. Karsten's mother held the wedding supper for them, and Louise's father was true to his word in providing the chickens.

As he had said, John Crozier did not attend the wedding, a fact that Louise regretted for many years to come. To her youthful way of thinking, if she was eighteen she didn't need his blessing or approval to get married. Decades later, she regretted that decision, realizing that if she and Karsten were meant to be together, they could have—should have—waited until her father could give his full blessing to the union. She has said that, if she had it to do over again, she would wait and that she would recommend that any young couple who plan on getting married wait for the parents' blessing.

For honeymoon money, Karsten sold his 1927 Model T Roadster to his brother for twenty-five dollars, then borrowed the car back for a week to drive on the honeymoon. He and Louise set out for the Solheim family's summer cabin in Suquamish. They spent a few more days in various small towns, finally heading back to continue their new life together.

About an hour from home, between Tacoma and Seattle, the engine of the old Model T began making a terrible racket. It sounded to Louise and Karsten as if the car was falling apart. Karsten pulled off to the side of the road, climbed underneath the car, removed the oil pan, studied the lower half of the engine, and realized the source of the noise was a bad bearing.

Having no spare parts, he walked to a nearby farmer's house and asked if they could spare a piece of bacon rind, which he cut into the right size to use as a temporary bearing. With that he bolted the parts together and started the engine. It sounded a lot better, and it carried them all the way back to Seattle, where he could work on it in earnest. Family legend says the bacon rind was crisp by the time they arrived at home.

Louise decided that she had married not only the most wonderful man in the world but a most ingenious one too.

LIFE CHANGES

Because of his marriage to Louise, Karsten's life had just undergone some radical changes. The changes continued soon after their wedding, when his father turned over to him complete control of the shoe shop Karsten had been running. It was now his business to run, not for his father, not with his father handling the ordering and paying the bills. It was Karsten's shop—lock, stock, and barrel.

Karsten had no experience running a business. He was good with his hands, and he was a good cobbler, but now he had to manage the business too. He had to pay the bills on time, order supplies and inventory, and otherwise keep the shop running smoothly. His father had paid him a modest wage, but now Karsten would have to see what was left over each month, hoping to net fifteen dollars a week for them to live on.

Their first five-room apartment cost $15.00 a month. Groceries were about $5.00 a week. They chopped wood for fuel, and Louise scrubbed the laundry on a washboard. The couple wasn't living "high on the hog," but they weren't starving, either. They were comfortable.

Like the other things he undertook, Karsten took seriously his responsibilities as a husband. He thought he had to do everything from running the business to buying the groceries. One thing he would not do, though, was any housework. Norwegian men didn't do housework, and he wasn't about to start.

As Louise got to know him better, there were more than a few surprises in store for her. She soon realized that, as busy as he was, he still craved activity. He always had to be doing something. After dinner every night, he wanted to go somewhere, anywhere. If he didn't have a church meeting, he would find somewhere else to go. But it wasn't long before much of Karsten's—and Louise's—time was taken up with a new role: that of parenting.

Louise gave birth to their first child, a son named Karsten Louis, in April 1937. And soon the couple and their son moved to the house that also was home to the shoe shop, where they would live for the rest of Karsten's shoe-repair career. In August 1938, Sandra Louise, the Solheims' only daughter, was born. She was a beautiful but sickly child who needed a lot of care, but she was also sweet spirited and much like her father in seeing no one as a stranger. Allan Dale came along in March 1940.

If there is one thing that will change a married couple's lives, it's having a child. Now the Solheims had three, and they were suddenly so busy with so many mouths to feed that life took on an entirely different pace.

Karsten and Louise traded off baby-sitting and attending church meetings. She might watch the children one night while he went to prayer meeting, and the next night he would watch them while she went to a young people's meeting. That worked until Louise decided it wasn't a good idea to have Karsten take care of the kids. It wasn't that he was unwilling or that he didn't care. He was just so tired that she would often come home and find him asleep on the couch while the toddlers tore through the house.

MOVING ON?

The Solheims had few material possessions and even fewer prospects for more. Karsten believed it was his responsibility to provide for his family, so he took government contracts that meant more work and smaller margins but a few more dollars. It wore him down, but he fulfilled his responsibilities even if it meant pulling a few all-nighters.

At times Louise wondered if his natural curiosity and ingenuity were being wasted at the shoe-repair shop. She respected his work as a cobbler, but she also believed there were other things he could be doing, things that would better use his gifts and talents. She didn't want to badger him or suggest he could be doing better for himself or for her and the children. All she cared about was whether he enjoyed what he was doing. She believed a person needed to enjoy his work to feel fulfilled in life.

Karsten had never spoken of bigger or different goals since he had proposed, but once Louise asked him, "Do you really like what you're doing?"

He ran a hand through his hair and sighed. "Well, I always try to do my best on every pair of shoes," he said. "That gives me satisfaction."

His answer fell far short of saying he enjoyed what he was doing, but his wife didn't pursue it. She believed he was capable of much more, but she was not in the least unhappy. In fact, she was as happy and content as she could be. She had only one Sunday dress, but that was life at that time. Few other people had anything, either, and people learned to be content with what they had.

One time when Louise needed a new dress, she went shopping but couldn't decide among the three she found at a local store. She took them all home to show Karsten so that he could help her choose, planning to return the other two. Instead, he told her to keep all three. She felt like the richest woman in the world.

But better days were ahead, due to what seemed only a quirk of fate, shortly after their third child was born.

6

NEW HORIZONS

Moving Onward and Upward

Life in the '30s and '40s wasn't easy for Karsten and Louise Solheim, but it was very good. They weren't rich by any materialistic definition of the word; in fact, they barely got by. But that didn't mean they weren't happy. They didn't have a lot of possessions, yet they were content with what they had. They had enough to take care of their three children and themselves, and they were grateful for what they had.

And they were happy with one another.

Karsten and Louise knew about friends or acquaintances whose marriages had been disappointing and who were unhappy, and he would say, "If anybody is the right kind of a person, there's no reason why he shouldn't be happy." Later, he would amend that statement to say, "God doesn't change, so it must be they changed."

To Karsten Solheim, being the right kind of a person meant doing everything with all your might. In his relationship with his family, in his work, in his personal relationships, his motivation was to serve God, and he tried to do everything as if for Him.

That attention to doing things the best he could was a huge part of what made him the giant in the golf industry he would one day become. And it showed in how he ran his business when he and Louise were first married. He wasn't one to do just the minimum to get by. Rather, his approach was to do the best he could on every project he worked on. To him, there were no "big" or "small" projects. All of them deserved his full attention and his best effort.

A DIFFERENT APPROACH TO BUSINESS

Karsten's craft of shoe repair was not a lucrative one, but it required diligence, skill, and an attention to detail nonetheless. He became very, very good at it, too. He evaluated the needs of a particular pair of shoes, set about repairing them as thoroughly and expertly as he knew how, and spent all the time and energy each required to do the job the best he could do it. He never wanted one shoe on which he could have done a better job to go back to a customer. He wanted to know—and he wanted his customers to know—that he did the best he could on a particular project. Not many years later he carried that same philosophy, work ethic, and attention to quality into golf-club design and manufacture, and the entire industry has never been the same since.

Karsten also believed in the old economic maxim "You get what you pay for." He believed, and has staunchly believed since that time, that if you make a superior product using superior materials, you can ask and receive a superior price for it. To paraphrase another old saying, if you build a better mousetrap, people will beat down your door to pay a better price to get one.

One of his favorite stories of his early years in shoe repair concerned a nearby competitor who dropped his prices to try to steal a little of Karsten's business. The shops were located close to one another, and both had been replacing leather heels on ladies' high-heeled shoes for twenty-five cents. The leather cost about half that, so the rest covered overhead and profit.

One day Karsten noticed a sign in the competitor's window hawking leather heels for fifteen cents. Karsten, fearing lost business, quickly decided he could sacrifice profits on heels, too, if it meant keeping his regular customers from changing loyalties. He put a similar sign in his window, informing people he had lowered his price on heels. Not long after that a customer asked, "What's the difference with your new heels? Not as good as they used to be?"

Of course they were every bit the quality they had always been, but Karsten was at a loss for words. What could he say? "It's just a sale," he said. That same day another customer asked the same question.

Soon it occurred to him that customers equated lower prices with lower-quality work, the logic being that if you pay less you get less. That may have been faulty logic in this case, but it was the way people took his lowering prices. He hadn't changed one thing about the way he did the leather heels except the price, and all he got for that was people asking if his workmanship had suffered and if he was using cheaper materials. As soon as he had a moment, Karsten took the sign out of the window and raised his price even higher than it had been before. He knew he bought better leather and was a more skilled and meticulous cobbler than his competitor, so his sign offered leather heels for thirty cents.

Now the questions from customers changed: "Why do your heels cost more than at the shop down the street?" Karsten was ready with an answer. He laid a quality piece of leather on the counter and encouraged customers to run their hands over the hide. "You tell me," he'd challenge the customer. "Surely we charge the same for labor. Must be we use a higher grade of leather." To his knowledge, he didn't lose a customer.

That day, Karsten Solheim learned a valuable lesson that permeates Karsten Manufacturing Corporation to this day: People will pay for quality products made with quality materials manufactured by skilled workers. Never again would he lower his price to try to gather more customers, not as a shoe-repair man and not as a golf-club manufacturer. He knew that the customer would be better served if he produced the highest-quality products possible using the highest-quality materials and charged an appropriate price.

It's an economic fact that, when you want a higher-quality product, you have to pay a higher price. It's that way with clothes, cars, homes, and any other item. It's that way with golf clubs. Custom-made golf clubs are not cheap. Golfers who buy on the basis of price have many sources, including discount department stores with sporting goods departments.

Karsten believed from the beginning that golfers who buy on the basis of quality would learn to come to him first. He knew that his clubs were a superior product, and he knew that it was only fair for him to charge what they were worth as compared with other clubs. It was a successful strategy, too. Just as people came to his shoe shop to pay a higher price for his heels, people have come to Karsten Manufacturing for his clubs for more than forty years. As a result, Karsten Solheim became an icon in the world of golf.

But before he would take his place at or near the top in golf-club manufacturing, Karsten would make several changes in his professional life. He would also take his family on an odyssey that moved them an incredible eighteen times in his and Louise's first twenty years of marriage. The first change in vocation occurred after a minor freak injury he suffered during some recreation.

A CHANGE IN DIRECTION

Karsten Solheim's is a true American success story involving a man who came from a humble background as a motherless child, then a cobbler, to become one of the most successful businessmen in the nation and one of the best-known figures in the sport of golf. But how did he come out of virtually nowhere to get to the top of the golf world after such a beginning? It's an amazing story filled with twists and turns along the way, and, oddly enough, it involved some time selling cookware.

Karsten had much to learn about being a businessman before he would be able to start his golf-club business. Leaving the shoe-repair business and becoming a salesman was necessary for his development as the consummate businessman. Cookware just happened to be the catalyst to move him out of the shoe shop toward bigger and better things.

It took a freak accident to make Karsten even think about a change in careers. He fell and sprained his wrist while ice-skating, making it impossible for him to hammer shoes for several weeks. There was no accident insurance to fall back on in those days, and the Solheims had no savings to draw on while he recovered from the accident. If he couldn't work, his family wouldn't eat or have a home to live in. Karsten wasn't going to have that. He knew he had to do something for income during the downtime, and, as was Karsten's way, he had become fascinated by a new idea: an innovation in cookware.

Karsten and Louise were invited to a couple of parties

where a salesman cooked an entire meal in aluminum alloy pans manufactured by Advance Aluminum Castings Corporation, makers of cooking utensils called Miracle Maid. This cookware was popular at that time. Housewives all over the country quickly became enamored of it. And Karsten, because of his inventive and inquisitive mind, was also drawn to the product. He wondered what allowed people to cook healthier foods without oils and grease and butter and even without water.

This cookware was like nothing he had ever seen, and he wanted to know how it worked before he started selling it. After talking to people who knew about it and examining it himself, he found the secret had something to do with the design of the lids. The bottom of the pan was heavier than the rest, and the lids fit tightly. The condensation caused by the proper temperature dripped from the top and aided in the cooking. Karsten loved the idea and the healthful benefits it afforded its customers. He was sold on the product. He wanted in on the sales.

In 1940 he left shoe repair and never looked back. He began selling Miracle Maid at parties. At first, his new line of work was hard on his family, both financially and because he was away from home so much. He was gone most evenings and much of the day as well. He had to learn to sell, and he was on commission. There was no guaranteed income for him. For the first year or so of selling, things were so tight for the Solheim family that for a time they moved in with Louise's father. That marked just one of the many moves they would make during the next several years.

But Karsten believed in the product he was selling. People seemed drawn to his humble friendliness, and he never lost his own fascination with the new technology. Soon he became more confident in his ability as a salesman, and business began picking up. Before long, he had become a huge success in sales with this new product. In fact, by his second year he was the top salesman for Miracle Maid on the West Coast. Soon the company's home office offered him a division managership in California. That meant a healthy salary of $40.00 a week, plus an overwrite on the sales of all his subordinates. It also meant moving his family to Fresno in the fall of 1941.

Louise was happy to move to Fresno, and she enjoyed the freedom of a little more income. Although she and the children missed Karsten when he was on the road, she was convinced that one day he would be home for good. She reasoned that as he moved up in the company, he would surely be able to spend more time at home.

She was busy raising their three young children, and the only glitch in her relationship with Karsten was that he sometimes disregarded her opinions. Fortunately, her opinions usually agreed with his, and while she may not have recognized his genius just yet, she was convinced he was an exceptional person. When they disagreed, he sometimes ignored her. Other times, when she came up with what she thought was a good idea, he would dismiss it as something "you must have read in a book."

Louise felt hurt that Karsten disregarded her ideas and opinions. At the same time, though, she knew his actions weren't due to any ill will or real anger at her. She had figured out that he wasn't as much hardheaded or disrespectful of her as he was a man with a one-track mind. If his one fault was that he wanted all his ideas to be self-generated, she decided she could live with that.

Those who came to know Karsten knew him as a man who had difficulty taking input from those around him. He never wanted to listen to others when it came to discussing how to do things, and he definitely didn't worry about the competition. He had learned that lesson the hard way in the shoe-repair business, and he wouldn't make that mistake twice.

Louise sensed Karsten was figuring out that the real money was in manufacturing. If the company could afford to handsomely reward its salesmen, then the owners—the makers of the products—were really the ones profiting. More than once he told her, "I want to think of something I can make that lots of people need." That would come later, of course, but for then, he was prospering by selling Miracle Maid cookware, and it seemed nothing could stop him—until the day Japanese forces bombed the United States military base at Pearl Harbor on the morning of December 7, 1941, dragging America into war.

At that point, the United States had managed to stay out of the two-year-old war in Europe, but when Japanese warplanes suddenly and without provocation attacked, killing thousands of United States servicemen, wounding many more, and sinking most of the Seventh Fleet, the "Sleeping Giant" had been awakened. The United States had no choice but to go to war.

Thousands upon thousands of American men were called on to serve their country in both the Pacific and European theaters, and those who were left behind to work faced changes in their jobs. Many manufacturers had to change their focus to help with the war effort. And as it had for many American businessmen, life changed drastically for Karsten Solheim.

CONTRIBUTING TO THE CAUSE

On December 8, the day after the attack on Pearl Harbor, the Miracle Maid division managers received telegrams from the home office informing them that all they had to sell was whatever the company had in stock, and a list of that stock was included in the letter. Aluminum had become a priority material for the military, and no more could be used for the production of domestic goods until the end of the war.

The "end of the war" seemed right around the corner every week and month for years, but meanwhile Karsten had to generate an income. When the Miracle Maid stock was depleted, there was no more work, no more money. The Solheims had been in California less than two months, and now it was time for Karsten to figure out another way to support his wife and children.

The local newspaper advertised the military's need for engineers or anyone with an engineering background. Engineering had always fascinated Karsten, despite just a year of college under his belt at the University of Washington. The University of California offered a ten-week extension course in engineering at Fresno, and he enrolled in it.

As soon as Karsten began that short course, he knew he had found his niche. The principles of engineering seemed to come to him as naturally as breathing. One day, the professor had a problem that he said couldn't be solved. Karsten insisted he could solve it, so the professor told him to go ahead and solve it. Karsten did just that. He was so far ahead of the rest of the class that, halfway through the course, he was encouraged to quit and go immediately to San Diego and begin work for Convair (now General Dynamics), where a job was waiting for him. It was a government job working on airplanes.

In April 1942, the family moved to San Diego, but Karsten soon felt he was being underpaid. He took a job in National City, south of San Diego, where he worked for the shipyard. They had a government contract for twenty-two concrete ships. The steel ones took too long to build, so a steel superstructure supported a pouring of concrete that was somehow buoyant enough to float.

Time was of the essence, and one day Karsten invented a tool that helped workers bend steel more quickly and efficiently. The company instituted a suggestion policy where employees could win a prize each week for the best idea. After Karsten won the first several in a row, they ruled that a person should not be entitled to win more than one prize each month. Karsten protested that as unfair. Finally it was announced that suggestions could be submitted from employees identified by codes, so that no one would know who had submitted them until the code was deciphered. Karsten won several more and had never felt so productive.

He enjoyed the work he was doing, but it took its toll on his time with his wife and children.

BALANCING FAMILY AND WORK

Karsten worked twelve-hour days, seven days a week, and the family seldom saw him. He loved the challenges and the work, but his children were usually asleep when he returned home.

When Karsten was present, he expected the children to behave. Once he caught Lou saying a bad word and disciplined him for it.

"Well, what *can* I say then?" Lou asked.

"You can say anything you hear me say," Karsten told him.

One Sunday, when Karsten thought he had the day off for once, the shipyard called and wanted him to come in. "What in the Sam Hill do they want me for today?" he complained.

Lou had heard him. "Now I can say, 'What in the Sam Hill'!" he exulted.

Once Lou told Karsten, "Daddy, I would never tell you to sell Mother, because she buys us ice cream every payday!"

They had a laugh over that, but it made Louise realize how many times she'd had to tell the children, "Wait till payday."

Once, when the family was at the christening of one of the ships Karsten had worked on, a man noticed beautiful, four-year-old Sandra. He smiled at Karsten as he passed and said, "I'd give you a thousand dollars for that little girl."

Karsten smiled his thanks and shook his head, and Lou piped up, "Daddy! Why didn't you take it?"

ANOTHER CHANGE

In 1943 Karsten received papers from Seattle requiring him to report for the military draft. Just before leaving, he told Louise he liked the San Diego area and wanted to look around for a place to work there after the war was over. He checked with the people at Ryan Aeronautical Company, which had built Charles Lindbergh's famous *Spirit of '76*.

The people at Ryan liked Karsten's résumé and insisted on interviewing him right then for a job. He told them he had been asked to report for the draft. They said, "Do you have children?"

"Three," he said.

"We've never lost a father yet," they said and went to bat for him with his draft board.

He was awarded a deferment and immediately went to work for Ryan Aeronautical. The move would prove providential in his journey toward greatness.

Karsten Solheim was an immediate hit at Ryan Aeronautical. He took to the work immediately, doing a first-rate job on everything assigned him by his superiors. They were impressed with him and that he seemed to be a "natural" at this kind of work.

One day he came to work to find his desk being moved down the hall. He hadn't asked anyone to move it and wanted to know why it was being moved. "Where are you going with that?" he asked. "I liked it where it was."

"You've been promoted," he was told. "We're lending you to the chief engineer."

Karsten knew he had to be the least educated man on the team. It seemed he was the least qualified to be promoted so quickly. Yet they soon gave him an engineer's rating, and he was almost immediately recognized as one of the brightest and most productive members of the staff.

The chief engineer drew him into the task force working on development of the first-ever jet fighter plane, the FR-1 Fireball. Soon Karsten was chief mechanical engineer on this new plane. He had the chance to meet many people on the job, including the test pilots. It was not unusual for the Solheims to entertain test pilots in their home, and the children were fascinated by their exploits. One pilot was later killed, and the Solheim children still remember their shock and grief more than fifty years afterward.

The FR-1 Fireball was first conceived late in 1942, and the Navy Bureau of Aeronautics called upon Ryan to assist in the design, development, and production of the new combat plane. The Fireball would combine the advantages of jet propulsion with the conventional piston engine and propeller. It was the United States Navy's first airplane to utilize jet propulsion. Ryan Aeronautical rushed the Fireball into production during the summer of 1945, hoping it would outperform any enemy fighter and serve as a possible means of countering the Japanese suicide plane attacks.

The Fireball fighter could be operated on either its jet engine alone or on the conventional piston engine with turboprop only, but for peak performance the two power sources were used together. The engine combination in the Fireball made it possible to operate a jet plane from an aircraft carrier.

Karsten and Louise had their fourth child and third son when John Andrew was born in late December of 1945. When John—who now serves as chairman/CEO of Karsten Manufacturing—was just six weeks old, Karsten was sent to the naval air base near Washington, D.C. The Fireball was to perform its final demonstration for the navy at the Patuxent River Air Base. By the time Karsten returned, John was three-and-one-half-months old.

It wasn't a situation Karsten liked, and it wouldn't be long before another change in careers was in the offing. The long hours, the time away from the family, all of the wartime work had also worn down Louise. With the war finally over, both were eager for him to get back into civilian work. On the way back to San Diego from Washington, he purposely had himself routed through Chicago so that he could check on things at Miracle Maid.

It was time for another turn along the road to greatness for Karsten Solheim.

7

MORE TWISTS AND TURNS

*Continuing the Journey
Toward Greatness*

The end of World War Two brought with it a demand for consumer goods by the American public. A great deal of the private economy had been turned toward the war effort, leaving many Americans without disposable income to purchase goods, and the goods themselves were scarce because industrial America was focused on the military effort.

Like many who worked in the defense industry during the war, Karsten Solheim found himself wondering about work in the nonmilitary sector of the economy once the war ended. Since he had experience and had been quite successful in selling Miracle Maid cookware, he decided to drop in to see if his former employers would remember him.

Of course, the people at the Miracle Maid home office

remembered Karsten well. Prior to the war he had been one of their top salesmen in the country. They knew him as a hardworking, conscientious salesman who also believed in their product. And they wanted him back on board with them, only this time in a higher position with the company than before.

Now that Miracle Maid products were back in production, the company needed someone just like Karsten to become the factory rep, a district manager, in California. He had been a division manager in California before going to work for Ryan, but now he would have several division managers under him in different areas of the state. His salary would be $75.00 dollars a week—a princely sum in 1946—and he would also make a commission on all the sales of his division managers and their subordinates. It was going to be a huge step up from where he was when he sold Miracle Maid products before.

Karsten's territory included all of California south of San Francisco, so in the fall of 1947 he moved his family back to Fresno. They bought a big house near Fresno State College and settled in. But it appeared that he would be busier than ever and away from home as much or more than before.

He set about rehiring the best salesmen he had had before, as well as many new ones. And as his job was recruiting, hiring, and training, he spent as much time on the road as most of the salesmen did. He showed them how to conduct the parties and sell the cookware. He was still sold on the product, and because people had gone so long unable to buy material goods, it was a seller's market. The product virtually sold itself, and Karsten again was very successful.

Louise wrote to her father and told him she had a house that would serve her children all the way through college, because they were right down the block from Fresno State. Her father wrote back that she should consider attending there herself. She loved the idea, but she decided to wait until John began kindergarten. She didn't realize there were already childcare and preschool for the children or she might have started earlier.

Louise wanted to take her father's advice, but she didn't feel that the timing was right, so she waited.

A TIME OF SEPARATION

In 1949, the Advance Aluminum Castings Corporation, which manufactured and marketed Miracle Maid products, decided to use its best man to open a new territory in St. Louis. Karsten was tabbed as the perfect candidate. Louise didn't want to take the children out of school and move that far away until he had survived the risk and gotten settled. Karsten was gone for a year, returning only for Christmas.

Even though Karsten was making great money for the time, the expense of maintaining two households was a strain for the family. It required Louise to double up the children in the bedrooms so that she could rent out a few rooms to college students. She provided board for them, too, and the first few months of that arrangement, she barely made ends meet. One of the boarders was a football player who nearly ate up her food budget.

Allan, nine years old, went to help at a Christmas tree lot, helping set up trees. He came home Christmas Eve with the sorriest excuse for a tree you've ever seen. To Louise, though, it was a beautiful tree.

To save money, Louise bought a live turkey. She had tried to wring the necks of many a chicken in her day. They had just stood up, shaken their heads dizzily, then staggered away. But she had never tried to behead a turkey. She couldn't get it to hold still on the chopping block and wound up whacking off half its head. When she caught it, it scratched her arm so deeply that it left a scar. She finally finished the job, dipped the turkey in boiling water, then spent hours plucking it, including the pinfeathers. She had saved a bit of money, but it wasn't worth the effort, and she resolved to never again buy a live turkey.

Later that night, Karsten made it home from St. Louis, and he brought a huge, one-dollar Christmas tree with him. He was not home long enough to suit wife or children, however. Before long he was back on the road again, working.

A FAMILY BUSINESS

While Karsten was gone, Louise served as a sort of district manager in absentia. The area Miracle Maid salesmen dropped off their orders to her, and she dispatched them to Chicago. She also wrote a weekly newsletter and sent it to all the salesmen in the district. Occasionally, sales meetings were still held in the Solheim home.

Once all the children were in school, Louise took her father's advice and worked in a semester of college, which she loved. Her college boarders warned her that she had been away from the classroom and wouldn't remember how to study. But she got all A's and B's and outdid her younger friends. She was required to go out for sports but was usually chosen last because she was older. She enjoyed proving herself in volleyball and badminton. Unfortunately, the Solheims would not be staying long enough for her to finish a degree.

Meanwhile, for all the pain and agony of separation for Karsten and his family, the St. Louis experiment had not been worth it. People were less willing there to open their homes for parties, especially since Karsten was a stranger. In Washington and California, he had started with friends and relatives. He didn't have that advantage in Missouri, so he had to start from scratch. It didn't work out, and after a year he returned to Fresno.

ANOTHER CAREER MOVE

The company had a policy stating that the salesmen were not to sell by pictures. The customers were to see the real article, and that meant the salesmen had to cart around two huge, heavy suitcases full of cookware. Karsten was convinced he could cover more territory and increase sales if he could leave that baggage in the trunk of the car.

Who could argue with more sales? Karsten reasoned. He had photographs of the cookware taken, and in 1950 began selling that way. His sales were astronomical, but before he could sell the company on the idea of at least considering a change in its policy, one of his own men turned him in to his superiors.

His salespeople had not been the same since he had left. Perhaps it was jealousy. Maybe they were after his job. Nonetheless, word got back to Chicago that Karsten Solheim was breaking the rules by selling with pictures, and he was fired. He had been the best salesman in Washington, then on the West Coast, then in the country while managing half of California. He had failed in Missouri but had succeeded "like gangbusters" upon his return to California, yet it was over. The company would not bend its rules, even for someone who had served it so well. Karsten's way was working, but he was still out of a job.

For Karsten, though, this was good timing, since his skills and talents were again needed to assist in a war effort—this time the Korean War. After about a five-year second stint with Miracle Maid, it was back to the defense industry for him.

BACK TO ENGINEERING

The Korean War was escalating, so Karsten immediately went back to engineering. Ryan Aeronautical brought him back to San Diego in 1951, but despite the Korean conflict, after a few weeks at Ryan it became clear there was not enough work for him there. He hired on again at Convair and worked on the Azusa Project, the first ground guidance system for the Atlas missile to be installed at Cape Canaveral (now Cape Kennedy).

This was a time when, at long last, Karsten was able to be home with his family more than before. He was home more than he or Louise could remember. Young John, now five years old, was unaccustomed to his father being home so much. After about two weeks, he asked his mother, "How come Daddy's home every night now?"

Although Louise was glad to have Karsten home for her and the children, it was also a time when there seemed to be strain in their marriage. Karsten, never one to be overly talkative, even at his best, seemed more distant than ever. She thought that perhaps he was still brooding over losing his position as factory representative for Miracle Maid. Whatever the problem was, there were times he seemed almost a stranger to her.

She soon went to work outside the home for the first time, putting her knowledge of math and science to work at Convair. She worked as an assistant to the engineers who were doing tests on airplanes in the wind tunnels. She plotted the results of the tests in graph form for them on simulated tests for experimental aircraft. It was a time when Louise felt grateful for her father's making her take so much math in school. Both she and Karsten had top secret clearance at Convair.

Within a year after Karsten started working at Convair, the foreman on the Azusa Project left, and Karsten was put in charge of it. The first thing he did was to halt the work. He was called in to answer for that. "Why have you stopped the project?" his superiors asked him. "Because I've studied it, and what they were doing won't work," he said, and then he convinced the brass he could make it work another way. He did just that, too.

By 1953, however, Karsten felt he was being under-paid, considering his contributions to Convair, and he asked for a raise. When the company turned him down, he started looking for another position with another company.

A GOLF GAME OF DESTINY

In the paper Karsten saw an ad from General Electric, announcing that a company representative would be in town interviewing potential employees. He went down-town to find the recruiter and was almost too late. In fact, he *was* too late for an interview at least, as the interviews had been scheduled. He was told that the interviewer had already checked out of the hotel and was on his way out the door.

Karsten hurried, caught him before he left, and asked if they could at least chat. Fortunately, the man agreed to talk with him. The recruiter told Karsten he was looking for personnel for their advanced electronics laboratory in Itha-ca, New York, which worked in conjunction with Cornell University. Karsten was intrigued by the opportunity, and the recruiter was impressed with him. Two weeks later, he was offered a job as a mechanical design engineer on so-phisticated radar and other electronic guidance systems.

He accepted the job, and the family was in for yet an-other big move.

Karsten went on ahead and moved to Ithaca in March 1953 to start his new job. Louise stayed back to get the children out of school and sell the house. It marked the be-ginning of what would be a fourteen-year relationship be-tween Karsten and General Electric.

Louise had begun attending college again when her own work slowed, and she had completed much of the first semester at San Diego State College. She had to drop much of her full load the second semester because she couldn't handle the job, the children, and the house on her own. Besides, Karsten had taken out a loan to finish a basement bedroom and add a bathroom in their house, and she had to supervise that also. She and the children didn't join him until August.

Karsten was in on the ground floor of the technology that has made everything smaller for the last several decades. He was intrigued and motivated by his interesting work, but once again he had been separated from his family. With his love for people, he looked for social activities. That summer, before Louise and the children were able to join him, he accepted an invitation from some colleagues to play golf. He accepted eagerly, not telling them he had never played the game.

Though he had bought a set of clubs for two dollars at a garage sale years before, they had sat in a closet, and he had not brought them with him to New York. Luckily for him, the professor whose home he was renting had a set of clubs to loan. Karsten took them to the golf course with high hopes, not of winning or even competing, but for using his mind and his athleticism to at least cover the fact that he was a rank beginner.

There aren't many golfers around who haven't felt the humiliation of playing their first game with those who know how to play. It can be embarrassing to try to get the ball to go where you want it to. Karsten tried, and he failed. Though he had not expected to do well, he at least hoped not to embarrass himself. But embarrass himself he did. He was humiliated to be left behind at the first tee. His companions were standing on the second tee while he was still in the first fairway. He'd taken ten shots and hadn't even made the putting surface.

After that, things only got worse. Much worse.

Once he reached the green, Karsten found that his putting was even worse than his driving. No matter how he swung the putter, no matter how straight he hit the ball, no matter how perfectly he placed the ball on center of the putter head during his swing, the ball would go right or left—never straight. The ball tormented him each time he tried putting.

Karsten soon realized that putting was about half the game of golf, and he took to practicing. He got very serious about his putting. He practiced at home and on the course after work. He became almost obsessive about figuring out how to hit that little white ball straight so that it would go in the hole. He got somewhat better as he practiced, but he couldn't master hitting the ball straight, no matter what he did.

Finally, the engineer in him started to wonder how the flat blade of the putter could cause him to hit the ball first one way and then the other, when he was convinced he was using the same stroke. Karsten had no illusions about his game. He knew he wasn't a great golfer or even a good one. He was, after all, a beginner. But at the same time, he was irritated with the engineers, the designers, the makers of the clubs. It seemed to him that the putters golfers used were more of a hindrance to a golfer's game than an asset. That just didn't seem right to him.

Karsten examined his motive for any sense of defensiveness or excuse. Clearly many golfers seemed to master the use of these simple instruments. Many—particularly professional players—had learned to hit the ball straight and true time after time. Clearly, it wasn't an impossible endeavor. Still, he wondered if the common player, the beginner, and even the expert wouldn't enjoy the game more if it rewarded the player for his consistency and didn't penalize him for the clubs' inconsistencies.

He began applying his curiosity and his engineering craft to dreaming about a way to make a better golf club. He couldn't imagine there would be much profit in it, but still he wanted to consider it. What would make that club head, the blade of the putter in particular, remain steady and true and keep it from twisting when the golfer stroked the ball?

Reasoning like an engineer, Karsten thought about tennis rackets and how they are designed with all the weight on the rim. That kept the racket from twisting and turning in the players' hands, allowing them to have more control over where the ball went when they hit it. Without that weighting on the frame, hitting a fast-moving tennis ball would produce the same results as if you did it with a Ping-Pong paddle: There would be no control. He started to wonder if the same principle would work in a golf putter.

Was it possible the answer to his and others' putting woes was something as simple as adding a little weight to the heel and the toe of the blade? As the standard putter was made back then, it was merely a chunk of heavy metal at the end of a shaft that was at the mercy of the smallest movement of the hands. The club head might move first one way and then the other, and who knew how close it would be to square with the hole when it came into contact with the ball?

Surely there had to be a better way to make a club. If the club head, looked at from front or back, looked like a foot, then a little weight at heel and toe should stabilize it. Karsten wasn't sure how much time to waste thinking about it, but it certainly struck him initially as an interesting possibility.

A multimillion-dollar idea? That never crossed his mind.

He just wanted to be able to putt straight.

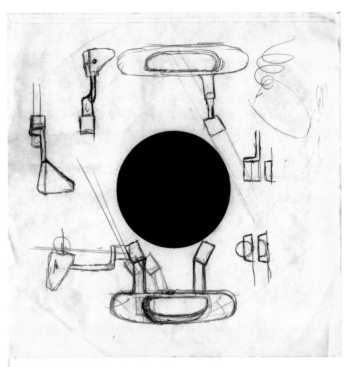

The original drawing for the PING Anser putter (1966) was done by Karsten Solheim on a 78 rpm record dust jacket. Always thinking, the inventor perhaps used the hole in the dust jacket as a substitute for a golf hole as he sketched ideas for his famous putter.

Karsten learned the shoe repair trade and early marketing lessons from his father. Karsten (pictured) went on to operate his own shoe repair shop in Seattle, Washington. Photo circa early 1920s.

Karsten demonstrates "heel-toe" balance to his young son, John. Little did they know that in 50 years, John would become the second PING president. Circa 1946.

Proud of their production of PING putters, Karsten and Louise lined them up at their Redwood City, California home for this historic photo.

Transferred by General Electric to its Syracuse, New York Electronic Park in 1954, Karsten helped design and build the cabinet and rabbit ears antenna to clamp onto GE's first portable TV.

While employed by Ryan Aeronautical Corporation as a flight research engineer, Karsten (center) worked on the Fireball jet fighter plane. Others pictured are Ed Sly (left) and Al Conover in this 1946 photo at Patuxent River, Maryland.

Karsten and son, John, with the PING Anser iron and PING Anser putter, circa 1967. John worked evenings, side-by-side with his father in the family garage while attending high school during daytime.

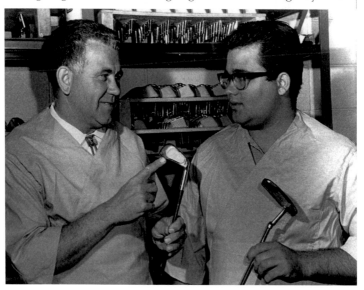

When not showing golf professionals his latest PING putter, Karsten enjoyed greenside chats with entertainers such as Bing Crosby.

Intent on making birdies with PING putters, comedian Bob Hope and Karsten often played in the Phoenix Open Pro-Am, once ending up on the winning team.

Karsten was a familiar sight around PGA Tour putting greens during the 1970s as his putter business began to grow. Arnold Palmer used a PING putter on several occasions during his career.

Walter Cronkite and Karsten confer on PING club-
making. The Solheims and the Cronkites have
become good friends since the Walter Cronkite
School of Journalism and Telecommunication has
been established at Arizona State University.

Top-rated radio newscaster Paul Harvey visited Karsten at his PING factory in the early 1970s. Karsten later became a sponsor of the Paul Harvey News radio network program.

Karsten presents a set of custom-fit, custom-built PING EYE2 golf clubs to Kareem Abdul Jabbar on his "retirement tour" from the National Basketball Association in 1989. Center-court at halftime of a Phoenix Suns-Los Angeles Lakers basketball game was the setting for the award.

Karsten received the prestigious Presidential "E" Award for Export Excellence from Ronald Reagan in a Rose Garden Ceremony at the White House in 1988. PING exports golf equipment to more than 80 countries.

Karsten enjoyed giving personal, behind-the-scenes tours of his PING plant, in this instance to Phoenix businessman Bob Simonds (left) and Vice President Dan Quayle.

A visit with President Bill Clinton in the Oval Office was a high-light for John Solheim (left) and Karsten and Louise, following an LPGA United States victory in the 1994 Solheim Cup.

The celebrated "Grooves Debate" of the late 1980s brought together Frank Hannigan (seated left), USGA Senior Executive Director, and Frank Thomas (USGA Technical Director) with Karsten and Louise at Moon Valley Country Club in Phoenix.

Karsten and Louise present The Solheim Cup to victorious USA team captain JoAnne Carner, at closing ceremonies at The Greenbrier Resort in 1994.

Karsten Solheim, a 5-handicapper in his prime, enjoyed playing in pro-am events, pictured here in the 1994 Phoenix Open Silver Pro-Am. He annually played in the Hawaiian Open Pro-Am on the men's tour, and the Standard Register PING on the ladies' tour.

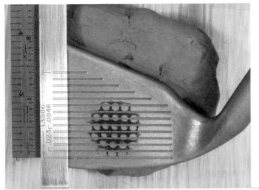

Measurement of grooves on PING EYE2 irons became the subject of a Karsten Manufacturing lawsuit against the United States Golf Association, which was settled out of court in 1990.

Karsten Solheim's PING Anser putter has become the most successful in the history of golf, accounting for more than 500 professional Tour wins. Its design still leads the industry in putters being sold today.

The year 1994 was an important one for the Solheim Family as Golfweek Magazine named Karsten "Golf Industry Father of the Year," and the National Golf Foundation named the Solheims as "Golf Family of the Year." Left to right are Louis, John, Louise, Karsten, Sandra and Allan.

Karsten and Louise Solheim celebrated their 50th wedding anniversary in 1986. Proverbs 3:5–6 was a guideline for their lives throughout their 63 years of marriage.

8

THE MAN WHO COULDN'T PUTT STRAIGHT

*Changing the
Face of Golf*

It's safe to say there are thousands of would-be, wanna-be golfers who have in frustration given up the game because they couldn't consistently hit the ball straight, because they couldn't get it to go where they wanted it to go. It's been said that consistently hitting a golf ball straight is one of the hardest things in sports to accomplish—maybe the hardest. (Some would argue that hitting a Major League baseball curveball deserves that spot.) Rather than face that frustration, many have relegated their clubs to dust-collecting status in the back of a closet.

Karsten Solheim had faced that particular frustration

and embarrassment for the first time when he was forty-two years old. Remember, his companions had to wait for him to catch up with them during his first attempt at golf. He'd had a hard time staying on the fairway when he teed off, but it was worse when he tried to putt. However, instead of giving up, Karsten took a look at his game and his golf equipment, then set about figuring out why he couldn't putt the ball straight. After that, he worked on solving the problem.

There was something in Karsten Solheim's emotional and mental makeup that wouldn't allow him to say, "I can't," but made him ask, "Why can't I?" That something then forced him to figure out what kinds of changes in his game and in his clubs would help him accomplish what he wanted to.

Because of Karsten's refusal to be defeated by a club, a green, and a little white ball, the game of golf has never been the same.

A STUBBORN RESOLVE

It's not likely that anyone who knew Karsten Solheim would deny that he was a stubborn man: not his employees, not his business associates, not his golf partners, and certainly not his wife and children. Not even Karsten would have denied that he was hardheaded when he pursued something.

In many settings, stubbornness of that kind can be a weakness, but in Karsten's case it turned out to be a strength. His obstinacy translated into a dogged determination to accomplish what he set out to do, no matter what it was, no matter what kind of effort and time it took on his part. When someone told Karsten Solheim that something couldn't be done, he didn't take it as a warning but as a challenge. In his mind, there was not an engineering or design problem that could not be solved, not a discipline or a sport that could not be mastered—as long as you had the patience to learn it and the kind of equipment you needed to succeed.

Not only did his initial humiliation at the game of golf get him to apply his mind to club design, but it also served to motivate him to master the game itself. He had never had time to become a great athlete, but he considered himself a sportsman nonetheless. Had he not had to work from a young age, he might have become a good football player or a better baseball player. It had not taken him long to become an excellent bowler and win the Syracuse city championship. (When he bought his ball, he drilled the finger holes himself.) He averaged higher than 190 and often rolled a 600 series. His game was just a few ticks shy of an average that might have put him on the pro tour.

Karsten's obsession with being excellent in his endeavors showed to a fault when it came to bowling. He had fallen in love with bowling, and he wasn't content to bowl one night a week. No, he bowled in three different leagues. He worked long hours, and just about any night he had open he spent bowling. This put some strain on his and Louise's marriage. She was not happy about her husband's being gone so much, and she told him so. She understood that he worked hard and needed recreation, but she wished he had taken up a daytime sport so that he could be at home in the evenings.

Like golf? That simple game where the object was to put the little white ball in the hole, hitting it as few times as possible with your clubs?

Oh, this game of golf! It appeared so easy and was yet so frustrating. Karsten got himself a set of clubs and began practicing every spare moment. He drove, he chipped, he putted. He still questioned the design of the clubs and continued to ponder what kinds of changes could be made to make them better. In his engineer's mind, he retooled the clubs thousands of times over, looking for the right design to make the game easier.

In the meantime, he became a very good golfer. Inside of four years he attained a five handicap (averaging five over par), breaking 80 consistently. He added a slew of golfing cups and trophies to his shelfful of bowling awards.

Karsten wasn't satisfied with becoming a good golfer, though. All his success on the course did was make him that much more determined to do something about the clubs that would make his—and everyone else's—game even more enjoyable. He reasoned that the more you could depend on the club to do what you wanted it to do, the better you would play and the more you would enjoy the game. That reasoning was what made him the success he became in the world of golf-club manufacturing.

But when would Karsten's ideas about improving golf clubs—putters, to start with—translate into action? How would he get started?

THE BEGINNING OF SOMETHING BIG

Louise and the children had joined Karsten in Ithaca in the fall of 1953, and she began working in the Engineering College at Cornell, computing heat transfer tests. Though she would never finish her education, she felt productive and knew she was learning things she might never have studied in class.

In August 1954, eighteen months after he'd arrived in Ithaca, General Electric moved Karsten and his family to Syracuse, where he was named project engineer for the first portable television. He designed an attractive, compact, metal cabinet to house the electronics. One sticking point to a smaller, lighter TV was the antenna. Conventional rabbit ears would be cumbersome to lug around. In designing the packaging of the TV, Karsten came up with several ideas to cut down the number of bolts and screws. He demonstrated how his design, even with fewer fasteners and thus much lighter than the first prototype, would be sturdier. He proved it by getting everyone's attention, then kicking the packaged TV down a flight of stairs. It survived in working order.

The best design idea Karsten had for the portable TV was a set of rabbit ears small enough to attach to the TV and even fold down so that the whole unit could be easily transported in one piece. He came home when the project had been completed and was on its way to the assembly line, and he complained to Louise. "They aren't too optimistic about it. They like it, but they just don't know if there's a market for portable television. They're going to test the national market with forty thousand units."

The company's lack of optimism—at least the way Karsten saw it—was unfounded. A few years later, when GE sold its two millionth portable TV with Karsten's attached rabbit ear design, they sent him a gold-plated model.

Karsten experienced great success with General Electric in Syracuse, but it was a personal project—almost a personal vendetta—that made him the man golfers around the world have come to know.

KARSTEN'S FIRST PUTTER

It was in Syracuse that Karsten got the idea of building himself a putter. He tinkered with the idea for a while before it became reality. Finally, he came up with a design he believed would work. It certainly wasn't much aesthetically. It was a simple blade putter. He made it out of a bar of aluminum.

Karsten had access to the design shop at work, and he began tinkering with the putter there, adding weight to heel and toe to give it more stability in his hands. From the sole of the putter he hollowed out space in the heel, inserting heavier metal to provide extra weight to heel and toe and give it the balance he had been looking for.

The design engineer at the shop kept telling him, "You can't do that here," referring to private, non-work-related projects. But when Karsten finished makeshifting his putter, the man changed his tune. He wanted one for himself. "Hey, make me one of those," he asked. Apparently he had his own frustrations on the putting green.

The results of Karsten's work were exactly what he had hoped for. While his putter was an ugly thing, it was nonetheless effective. The heel-and-toe weighting helped his golf scores begin to plummet. The weight did what he had expected it to do, and he was able to stroke his putts with much more accuracy and confidence. They rolled truer because the putter head stayed square when mishit.

After completing his putter, Karsten went to work on customizing his own set of clubs. He'd bought a set of new clubs through a pro friend at church. He liked how they felt in his hands, but when he tried them out, they were as disappointing as all the rest. He began experimenting with changing the weight distribution of those club heads as well. He had no idea where it would all lead, but he enjoyed the challenge of making something better. He drilled holes to displace weight and added soldered pieces of metal elsewhere for improved balance. They didn't look very pretty; they looked as if they had been through a war. But they worked better. His golf scores continued to drop.

Karsten was finding great success in his personal golf game using his new putter, but there was also a foundation being laid for his future business. In 1956 the U.S. Open was played in Rochester, New York, and Karsten got to see Ben Hogan play. Karsten didn't know it then, but the mere experience of getting to different courses and meeting local golf professionals was exposing him to a side of the business he could have learned no other way. He couldn't know he would one day be considered "The Emperor of Golf." He was an engineer by trade, a sportsman by hobby and avocation. He just happened to be applying his engineering skills to his hobby. Who knew what would come of it?

Karsten himself had no idea where his tinkering with his golf clubs would take him, but he soon found himself and his family taking another step toward greatness in golf manufacturing.

HEADING (BACK) WEST

With the TV project complete, Karsten wondered what was next. Both Karsten and Louise missed California. One day he came home and announced there was a rumor that GE was going to join the computer race, and it would be in California. Sure enough, a few days after the rumors started, Karsten learned they were true. He tracked down the man who was to head up the new computer division in Palo Alto. "What's the chance of my getting to go with you?" Karsten asked him.

"I have a spot for a man like you," he said. "But I can't talk directly to you about it. Protocol, you know."

"Then talk to my boss."

Neither Karsten nor Louise was crazy about living in New York, but moving so much and so often had not been easy either. At each new location, Louise made it her priority to find a Bible-teaching church with an active youth group. This way the children would get involved in church activities and make friends quickly. Karsten too had become active in the men's group at church. He also still worked at his golf game before work every morning and after work until dark.

In Syracuse the Solheims had purchased a seven-bedroom, five-bath home (for $21,000). The spacious brick house was too large for the average six-person family, but it gave Louise an opportunity. The mother of her best friend from childhood, Margie Cross, had taken in some foster children, and Louise longed to do the same. She knew what a loving family had meant to her when she was a girl, so she and Karsten welcomed two foster children, both girls—a seven-year-old and a fifteen-year-old—into their home. Though for the next decade they moved a lot, the younger girl was very troubled, and the older girl ran away with her boyfriend and got married, Louise has never regretted the decision.

In 1955, Louise had gone to work as a statistical technician for Eastern Milk Producers, a dairy cooperative headquartered in Syracuse. She enjoyed the job, which included travel to government milk hearings in Boston, New York, and New Jersey. She also worked as an assistant editor on the cooperative's monthly house magazine. She liked her work, and she felt appreciated on the job.

But it was time for another move. A few days after Karsten had asked about the possibility of transferring to California, the transfer was approved. They would be heading back West. The Solheims, minus Allan, who was with his grandfather Crozier, traveled cross-country in a 1956 Mercury station wagon with the other three children and the family dog and cat. Along the way they stopped in Chicago, where Karsten was invited to play at the beautiful Medinah Country Club. They also visited Yellowstone National Park and dropped Louis off at the University of Wyoming to continue his college career.

Upon their arrival in California, the Solheims lived in a motel in Palo Alto, waiting for their home in Redwood City to be built. Karsten had begun with General Electric's new computer department, only to discover that the national headquarters for the new division would be in Phoenix. Louise knew they should not grow too attached to their new home. Karsten worked on a project called ERMA, which was to be the first bank computer. GE and Bank of America were collaborating on it, and it would revolutionize the banking industry. He worked on the check sorter.

Karsten enjoyed his new work, and he continued getting better and better at golf. He practiced like a madman, chipping and putting in their Redwood City yard every spare moment he had. His son John would help him practice, standing at one end of the yard with a first baseman's glove to catch Karsten's chip shots.

He played at several municipal courses and began making a name for himself in local tournaments. On Fridays the golf pros in the area had their own little traveling Pro-Am tournaments, involving themselves and some of their better players at a different course each week. Karsten, with his five handicap, was always invited.

One of his favorite courses was Palo Alto Municipal Golf Club, because it was close to his work location. He played there often, and one day he had a conversation with the golf pro that changed the course of his life—and the game of golf. The pro, Pat Mahoney, complimented Karsten on his putting. "You're so consistent and confident," the pro said.

"You should have seen me before I made myself this putter," Karsten said. He showed it to Mahoney. He didn't point out what he had done to keep the putter head from twisting when it impacted the ball.

It didn't look like much to Pat Mahoney, and he didn't say a lot about what Karsten had designed, but what he did say got him thinking: "If you can make a putter that will roll the ball, rather than skip or slide it, you'll sell a million."

The typical putter in those days was simply a heavy piece of flat metal that swung like a pendulum at the end of the club shaft. No matter how smooth and careful the golfer was, when the club head met the ball, the ball left the face of the blade with no roll. It might jump. It might skid. But it rolled only after losing momentum and catching purchase on the green. By then it could be way off line, and any reading of the green a golfer might have done was rendered irrelevant. If the ball skipped or slid, it had more chance to roll in a wrong direction.

Mahoney said that the quicker a ball gripped the green and began to roll, the more control the golfer would have on the shot. And putting, as everyone knew, was what separated the men from the boys in golfing. It made little difference how long and true your drives and lofts and chip shots were if you didn't have a sound putting game.

Make the ball roll, Karsten thought. *The heel-and-toe weighting keeps the blade from twisting, but what would make the ball begin rolling as soon as it was struck?*

The engineer in Karsten started to take over again. He began mulling over how to design a putter that would contact the ball in such a way that it rolled off the face of the club, rather than jumping off. He hurried back to the office and began sketching a design. An idea had been born that would change his life, not to mention the game of golf, forever.

9

PING!

The Start of
an Enterprise

T his doesn't look like a GE job."

Indeed it wasn't. The machinist at the Kaiser machine shop, a vendor that supplied General Electric, looked at the sketch that Karsten Solheim presented him and immediately knew that what he was looking at wasn't from GE. In fact, it was nothing at all like anything he had worked on for GE.

It was a sketch that Karsten had worked on at home. It was a sketch of a golf putter. He had played with the angles, weights, and measures to try to figure out how to design the club so that it would make a ball roll off it instead of jump off when it made contact, thus keeping the ball rolling on the ground instead of skipping or bouncing. He had drawn and redrawn his idea until he was satisfied that it would work. Using his seemingly inborn understanding of physics and engineering, he designed a putter he believed would do what he wanted it to do and what Pat Mahoney said it needed to do.

It wasn't as aesthetically pleasing as most clubs of the day, but Karsten believed it would work better. It was composed of two parallel blades for the face of the putter with a torsion bar running between them. At each end of the blades—the heel, or back of the putter face, and the toe, the front of it—were weights to give the putter head stability in the golfer's hands. Initially, Karsten used a torsion bar to give him the effect he wanted. Later, he realized that all he had to do was design the club so that its weight was lower on the club head.

Pat Mahoney's suggestion that he design a putter that would keep the ball from bouncing or skipping on the green put a hook in him. It was another example of a problem that Karsten knew he could solve.

After satisfying himself that his putter design would work, he ran his sketch to the nearby machine shop and asked them to put it together for him. Karsten assured the machinist it wasn't a GE project, paid for the finished product with his own money, and hurried home to work on it some more. He put the putter head in a vise and drilled a hole in it for a shaft. After a few adjustments and more tinkering, his putter was ready to be greens tested.

The rest of the family hardly noticed as Dad went to the living room to try out this new putter. He had always practiced his golf game a lot, particularly since they had moved from New York to California, where the better weather gave him more opportunity to get outside. This was nothing new to them.

But it was new to Karsten. He found that his new creation worked even better than his first putter. As he had hoped, the ball rolled off the face of this putter instead of bouncing as it had with his first putter and with any other putter of that time. That, combined with the heel-toe weighting he had already implemented, gave the club a larger "sweet spot," allowing for a more forgiving club.

There was one unexpected effect of how Karsten had built his club. His design had left a hollowed-out space that made the putter a bell, and when the club struck the ball, the head emitted a high-pitched ring, not unlike the sound of a tuning fork. *Ping!* That gave him inspiration.

MAKING A NAME

Now Karsten wasn't just excited about how his putter performed. He was excited about the idea the club's musical tendencies gave him for a name. He was now seriously thinking about marketing the putter. But what would he call it? Right then, he dubbed it "the Ping putter."

Karsten rushed into the kitchen, where Louise was cooking dinner for the family, and excitedly announced his idea to her. "I have a name for my new putter. Listen to it *ping!* I'm going to call it the Ping putter."

"That's nice, honey," Louise said, not knowing where the idea would lead. She had grown used to his tinkering with the clubs, and she had other things on her mind at the time. She was more concerned with her growing family than with another of Karsten's new ideas.

They had been church shopping and found the Menlo Park Baptist Church, where Pastor Luther Plankenhorn's wife recognized the Solheim name and immediately informed them she had known Karsten when he was a child. That was enough to keep the Solheims in that small church, and Louise was grateful for everything it had to offer to young people. For one thing, it cooperated with the famed Peninsula Bible Church, pastored by Ray Stedman and a staff that included two young men named Charles Swindoll and Luis Palau. Swindoll went on to pastor one of the largest churches in California, become a radio preacher and best-selling author, and serve as president of Dallas

Theological Seminary. Palau became second only to Billy Graham as an international evangelist.

Only Karsten sensed he was onto something with his Ping putter. He knew he wanted to have a go at manufacturing the club and selling it. He had been thinking about that for some time. He believed that if golfers would give his new creation a chance, they would see their scores improve, and the putter would become a success for him.

The Ping 1A was ugly compared with others on the market at that time. But he knew that it worked, and if it worked, a golfer would all of a sudden find it a beautiful piece of equipment. Even if the golfer still thought it was ugly, he would likely overlook its lack of aesthetics. Karsten wasn't into aesthetics anyway. He was into functionality and practicality. And if his putter worked, he didn't care how it looked. He was getting ready to move his putter into the market.

Meanwhile, life was moving on. His eldest son, Lou, was going into his junior year of college, and his daughter, Sandra, was about to enter Simpson Bible College in San Francisco. Karsten hoped to involve the two younger boys, Allan and especially John (who would be at home several more years), in his fledgling side business, manufacturing and selling the Ping putter. Allan, graduating that year, was going into the United States Marines Reserves.

Karsten patented his design, then prepared to start producing the putters in the family home's garage in Redwood City. The first thing he had to do to get the garage ready was remove the wrecked carcass of a 1951 Kaiser that had been (dis)gracing half of the garage for more than a year.

In the winter of 1957, Louis had driven Allan and four other young men to San Francisco for a church-sponsored ice-skating party. On the return trip, traveling the Skyline Drive back to Redwood City, Louis was driving a little too fast for the curvy roads. He failed to make one of the turns, and the car flipped, throwing him and all five of his passengers out of the car (this was before the advent of seat belts). Fortunately, no serious injuries occurred, though all six young men had to go to the hospital to be examined. Louis called Karsten and Louise to tell them of the accident, assuring them over and over that no one had been seriously injured.

Karsten and Louise went to the hospital to pick up their sons and returned by the same route that Louis had taken to see the scene of the accident. They also returned the next day to see it by daylight. The Kaiser, flattened like a pancake, was totaled. For some reason, Karsten did not want the wreck towed to a wrecking yard but had it brought to the garage of their new home on Glennan Drive, perhaps to provide Louis with a reminder to drive more safely.

A year later, the entire family was glad to finally get the obnoxious, unsightly wreck out of the garage and to its proper graveyard. Thankfully for them, the new putter business made it necessary. From now on, the garage would be needed for production of Karsten's first putter, the Ping 1A, and its siblings.

GETTING STARTED

Right off the bat, Karsten would be doing things differently from most businessmen. When he started making putters, most of the golf clubs on the market were mass produced and forged. Karsten, on the other hand, would work on his clubs one at a time, and he would use sand casting to mold them. On top of that, he would use only word of mouth as his mode of advertising. His plan was to get golfers to try out his clubs, then let the results speak for themselves.

He decided to have the putters sandcast at East Bay Brass Foundry in Richmond, California, about an hour's drive from Redwood City. Initially he made them out of brass, but he quickly discovered that brass was too soft a metal, when a putter Arnold Palmer had ordered arrived with its face dented. Karsten couldn't believe it until Palmer showed it to him.

Karsten went to George Stewart, owner of East Bay Brass Foundry, who advised him to use manganese bronze, a much harder metal that lent itself well to sandcasting. Manganese bronze tends to darken with age, but Karsten didn't consider that a problem. Incidentally, East Bay Brass Foundry still casts the manganese bronze putter heads for Karsten Manufacturing.

Karsten decided it would be too expensive to job out the tooling on his putter heads, so he looked for his own milling machine. He found a used one listed in the newspaper for $1,100. His bank, The Bank of America of Menlo Park, told him they would lend him the money but not to expect any more loans. So, with no collateral other than his and Louise's signatures, he borrowed the money and purchased the milling machine. Afterward, Karsten always liked saying that $1,100 loan was the only money he ever had to borrow for his company.

Karsten moved his mill into the garage, which would enable him to make his own molds to cast the putter heads. He spent every spare moment producing the unusual, heel-and-toe-weighted putter that made the loud, ringing sound. He had no qualms about doing the tooling himself, although he had no previous experience in that area, other than being good with his hands. It was slow, arduous work, and he spent long hours late into the night making molds for his putters.

Immediately, the putter started to get attention, and that attention meant orders. *Sports Illustrated,* in its August 24, 1959, issue, treated the 1A as a novelty, announcing the invention of "a musical putter." A firm out East saw that and ordered a hundred putters to use as Christmas gifts. Suddenly there was an order big enough to require days of work. The Solheims still have photographs of the clubs that filled that order, which was by far the largest they had ever filled at the time. They laid out the clubs in their backyard, and John took the photographs.

From the very beginning, the putter business was a family affair for the Solheims. Karsten, concentrating mostly on John as his top assistant, taught his two youngest sons to help him manufacture the putters. They learned how to cut thin strips of cardboard for a foundation under the leather grips. They learned how to drill holes for the hosels (the socket in the club head where the shaft was attached). They used a heavy mallet to drive the shaft into the hosel. They learned about sandcasting. Sometimes dinner took a backseat to heat-treating putter heads, because they heated them on the burners of the stove top.

Karsten sought and received approval that his 1A putter conformed to the United States Golf Association rules of golf. He also had applied for the utility patent. At that point, his plan was to begin manufacturing on a part-time basis, turning out 100 putters a week. But he also had bigger plans. He hoped to expand production to 500 a week.

Most small businessmen—and this was a very small operation at the beginning—at that point would have spent a little cash to advertise their product, either in magazines or newspapers. They would have used some media outlet to make the public aware of their product. Not Karsten, though. In the beginning, his own words and the performance of the clubs were the only form of advertising he used.

He spent his spare time at golf clubs and pro tournaments. He hung around the practice greens, knowing that golfers with putting problems always turned up there. He was seen as an eccentric, a middle-aged man in worn shoes, trying to get everyone to try his funny-looking, not to mention funny-sounding, putter.

When on vacation or when just out driving around, every time the family passed a golf course, Karsten insisted on going in, finding the club pro, and demonstrating the Ping 1A putter. He set the retail price at $17.50, an unheard-of price. At that time, the best putters on the market could usually be found for less than $13.00 each.

The results in terms of sales weren't there at first. Although many people in the know predicted big things for the Ping 1A, there was resistance to the club. Even before he went into production, Karsten had several orders for the club, including twenty-four from the Paradise Valley Country Club in Phoenix. But large sectors of the golf public resisted the Ping 1A as something of a novelty and not a serious piece of golf equipment. Not only that, the Ping 1A was unsightly compared with the other putters of that day. Oftentimes, Karsten would take a putter to a golf club, only to come back several months later to see that it hadn't sold.

He continued to build and market his club his own way, not compromising on its price or on how he did his business. Once a golf pro tried the Ping and said he would use it if he didn't have to pay for it. Karsten refused. He believed that if the man really liked the product and saw the benefits, he should be willing to pay.

It was the same business philosophy he had used when he raised the price of heels in his Seattle shoe shop so many years before. It was the philosophy that if you have a higher-quality product made of higher-quality materials, you should be able to charge a higher price for it. He knew he had a quality product, a product that golfers around the world would eventually want—if only he could get them to try it out. He was determined to charge what the product was worth, and he wasn't going to resort to marketing through giving away his clubs. If someone wanted a Ping 1A putter in his or her golf bag, that person would have to pay what Karsten was asking for it.

REAPING THE REWARDS

In time, Karsten's way of doing business paid dividends. Interest in the club started rising in the golf world. Almost every golfer who saw the Ping putter wanted one, and those who used them saw their games improve. Soon the fame of the Ping 1A began spreading, mostly by word of mouth, and requests for the putter started coming in from pro shops as far away as Florida, New York, and Wisconsin, all without any advertising or marketing effort. Karsten added more molds to the line—2A, 3A, 4A, 5A, and 5B.

The Ping clubs were starting to become profitable, but both Karsten and Louise still considered the putter business a hobby, an avocation, something Karsten played at in his spare time. He was serious about it and convinced it could catch on, but his "real" job was as a mechanical engineer with General Electric. When GE asked him to spend six months in Schenectady, New York, for six months, it interrupted his side job.

People had begun buying the Pings. Though Karsten had done no advertising, a few pros had seen their putting improve with Pings, and word was getting around. The price—an otherworldly sum for a golf putter at that time—intrigued people. The reasoning appeared to be that if the club was that expensive, it must be something special. It developed its own little following, which proved mildly profitable for the Solheims. But Karsten's move to Schenectady nearly killed the Ping before it had a chance to take off.

ANOTHER TURN IN THE ROAD

Karsten's assignment in New York was another fascinating twist for him. He was to study cryogenics, which most people thought of as the process of freezing bodies until cures could be found for fatal diseases. General Electric had other ideas for its application. Karsten enjoyed the new field but was happy to go back to work on GE's ERMA project in partnership with the Bank of America and make a computer for the banking industry that would change banking forever.

When Karsten returned to California, he and son John jumped back into the putter business with enthusiasm. Though Louise worked at Ampex, a tape recording machine company in Redwood City, she helped with the business side of Ping. In the fall, when Louis went back to college, John became the only child remaining at home. Sandra had become a mail clerk at *Sunset Magazine,* and Allan had joined the Marines Reserves.

Karsten and Louise quickly grew tired of his constantly being shuttled between the GE lab in Mountain View, California, and their computer headquarters in Phoenix. Finally he pled his case to GE that it would be better for all concerned if he were transferred to Phoenix to cut down on the commuting.

In February 1961, they got their wish. GE transferred Karsten to Phoenix, and they began looking for a home in the Phoenix area. They wanted a house with a big garage and some acreage, space that would allow them to continue manufacturing putters without bothering the neighbors. They found the perfect place in Paradise Valley, just outside the city limits, on two-and-a-half acres.

The Solheims had lived in Redwood City for five years, and during that time Karsten had begun to establish his name in the putter business, introducing not only the Ping 1A but also several other models to the market. Already, the clubs were making money for the family. Now they were moving to Phoenix, where Karsten Manufacturing, which wasn't even in existence at that time, would one day flourish and make Karsten one of the most successful golf manufacturers in the United States.

Looking ahead to that kind of success, one might think

that all was well with the family. But there were troubles—troubles and opportunities for personal and spiritual growth for both Karsten and Louise.

10

A SEASON
OF GROWING

*In the Midst
of All This*

People who knew Karsten and Louise Solheim were constantly amazed at the love the two had for one another, and they were amazed at how that love spread to the couple's children and their families.

Even after more than sixty years of marriage—an incredible length of time, considering that we live in a day where there is one divorce for every two weddings—the love of Louise Solheim for her husband showed in her words and in her deeds. Her eyes still light up after all these years when she talks of him as "the most wonderful man I've ever known." She played a vital role in Karsten's success.

And Karsten, who in his late eighties could barely communicate verbally because of his battle with Parkinson's disease and associated conditions, was a different man when his beloved wife was near him.

It wasn't always easy for the Solheims. It was a deep love, but not a perfect love. Their relationship endured through some extremely tough times. The love—that very real and very enduring love—that Karsten and Louise shared, even into their eighties, helped them persevere through some unbelievable testing, the kind that might tear apart most people's marriages.

Yet, through everything, Karsten and Louise grew closer. During the course of their more than six decades together, they underwent oftentimes painful personal growth. And, somehow, their love grew stronger through everything.

A VERY TRYING TIME

Nineteen fifty-eight would prove one of the most difficult years of the Solheims' lives together. Louise had quit a job at Lockheed late in 1957 to take care of her ailing father, who had been diagnosed with pancreatic cancer. His care and his death in January 1958 stretched the family budget to the point where Louise had to tell Sandra they couldn't afford to send her back to Simpson Bible College for a second semester.

Sandra was upset about that, but then word came that an anonymous donor had paid her tuition for the second semester. She was able to go back. Then, in February, Lou announced that *he* was dropping out of college. Karsten and Louise were frustrated but didn't know what to do. They couldn't and didn't try to force him to return, praying he would come to his senses. He later did return to finish his degree and in 1960 would marry Bonnie MacDonald.

But if Louise thought 1958 had started with difficulties, had she known what was coming, she would have welcomed as benign the decision of a son to temporarily drop out of college. This dark time in the life of the Solheims came just prior to the final development of the Ping putter.

It was a time when Karsten wanted to focus on his new project, but it was also a time when one of their children desperately needed his and Louise's love and support.

During that year, Karsten and Louise's lovely, intelligent, talented, spiritual daughter, Sandra, suffered what they found out was a nervous breakdown. They first recognized the problem when Louise picked her up for Easter break. She had always been close to Sandra, but for some reason it seemed that day that Louise hardly knew the girl in the car with her.

Sandra laughed hysterically at things that weren't funny, things no one else could see. She waved at people on the street, assuming they had been waving at her, but hadn't. She told her mother the people were talking to her, and she answered them from inside the car. She said she knew things that no one else knew. Most alarming to Louise was Sandra's insistence that God had told her that big things were about to happen and that she would be part of them. Sandra had always been very spiritually tender, but Louise didn't understand a word of this.

That evening when Louise talked to Sandra, her daughter seemed in a trance. She stared into space, not answering, seeming not to hear. Suddenly she said that she was tired and went to bed. Louise recalled a neighbor's saying in September, after Sandra had baby-sat for him, that she seemed "spaced out." She had never seen that in Sandra and soon forgot about it. Until now.

Later the dean of women at Simpson called to speak with Louise. The dean told her that Sandra hadn't checked out of school and that her behavior at college had been quite bizarre. The dean also said that Sandra would need a clean bill of health before she came back to school.

Louise took Sandra to the doctor the next day. He recommended she see a friend of his who was a psychiatrist in San Francisco. Louise made an appointment to see him with Sandra. The strange behavior continued, and Louise began to worry even more. Then the psychiatrist saw Sandra and explained that she had had a nervous breakdown and needed to be hospitalized as soon as possible.

Louise was torn. She'd had a second cousin who wasn't treated for mental illness soon enough, and she wound up having to undergo shock therapy. That left her in what Louise saw as a vegetative state. She would not allow that to happen to their daughter. She wanted to get help for Sandra and even see that she was admitted to the hospital, but she knew Karsten would never allow it. He was hard on doctors to begin with, and he would certainly be even worse with psychiatrists.

Louise made the decision herself, right then and there, and had Sandra admitted to the hospital. She then went home and told Karsten. He was furious. He couldn't understand how or why Sandra needed to be admitted to a hospital, especially for this kind of problem.

The psychiatrist wanted to meet with both Karsten and Louise, but Karsten wasn't at all enthusiastic about the idea. Several days later, reluctantly and under protest, he went with Louise to see the psychiatrist. Karsten demanded to know what was wrong with his daughter, what was being done about it, and how quickly she could come home. The doctor told him, "We don't know what causes these things. But it has happened, and there are medications we can and are using. Our goal is to get her out of here as quickly as possible."

Karsten had a hard time understanding all this. He loved his daughter, and he couldn't understand how she had gotten to this point. What could have caused this? How could this otherwise healthy young woman have gotten to a state where she had to be hospitalized? Was it something Louise had done? It was more than he could deal with at the time.

Three weeks later, Sandra was allowed to come home, but Louise decided she was worse, if anything. In another three weeks she was too much to handle, and Louise took her back to the psychiatrist. Sandra was readmitted for four months, and Karsten and Louise were informed that a prerequisite to her release was family therapy.

THE STRUGGLE

Karsten, independent and tough-minded Karsten, didn't like the idea of family counseling at all. He was an old-school thinker, and he believed that the family should be able to work out its problems without the help of any psychiatrists or counselors. He would go but only against his will and with huge reservations. Louise, on the other hand, actually looked forward to family therapy.

Karsten resisted the therapy, complaining to Louise about it and actually refusing to go at one point. But he went often enough for Louise to learn some things about this brilliant man that she had never really considered before. It was a struggle for both of them, but it was also a time when she grew to understand and love Karsten all the more. She became more aware of his shortcomings, but she also began to understand how his upbringing and background had made him what he was. She had seen early that Karsten was a gifted man. Now she saw more deeply into him. He was a good man, a man of impeccably high character. He was a loyal man who believed in treating people around him fairly in every way. He loved God and his family, and he genuinely cared about people.

Karsten wasn't perfect in how he related to his family. He was away from home a lot, either working, playing golf, bowling, or working on his clubs. He wasn't an especially communicative person, and his wife often felt that he didn't appreciate her or respect her opinions. He wasn't a man who was easy with compliments or praise. For example, Louise had become a very good cook in her years with her father, and she loved cooking for Karsten. But he seldom, if ever, said anything complimentary about her efforts. She even once asked him if he liked something she had prepared, and he said, "It's fine. I'll tell you when it isn't."

Karsten was stingy with praise for his children too. He loved his kids, and he recognized good things they did at school, at church, wherever. But like his own father before him, he was never one to let them know when they had done something well. He would often brag to Louise about things they had done. She would ask him why he wouldn't tell the children he was proud of them, himself. He told her, "I always want them to feel that they could have done better."

In a nutshell, that was how Karsten drove himself, and that was how he drove his children. His philosophy in life was that he could always do better, no matter how well he had done something. If he rolled a 200 in a game of bowling, he wanted to beat that next time. He always wanted his next golf game to be better than the last. And, later, if he designed a good putter, he wanted to design a great one.

Louise knew that it would take a huge effort to stick with this man she loved and make their relationship successful, but she decided he was worth it. Despite his shortcomings in relating to her and the children, he was still a wonderful man.

A BREAKTHROUGH

During that time of family counseling, a true breakthrough took place for Karsten and Louise. After a period of cold silence, he changed in how he related to his wife. One day, he was just different. He seemed to change every day. He was actually trying. He was gentler with her. He asked her opinion. He might not admit a wrong, but he stopped short of pressing his points. He seemed to rely on her more, include her in decisions. It was as if he had discovered her value for the first time since their courtship.

After that time, Karsten and Louise went on to share a happy, loving, productive life together, working side by side in their ministries, in their personal relationships, and in the founding and growth of a large golf equipment manufacturing company.

The children also seemed to have survived—even prospered—after the tough times with the family. Lou became a successful entrepreneur in his own right, and he is an independent thinker. Sandra speaks openly about her nervous breakdown and, although she knows her limitations, has become a hard worker and very devout in her faith. Allan, whom Louise always felt Karsten had been too hard on, credits his father with teaching him that he was good with his hands. All four of the children work for Karsten Manufacturing.

John, who in essence grew up in the fledgling Ping business and now runs the company, recalls his father's being hard on him and wondering what it would take to please him. And yet he also has fond memories of apprenticing under his dad and learning discipline and perseverance as he learned how to succeed in the golf equipment business.

11

A FAMILY BUSINESS

*Taking a Place
in the Industry*

Looking around the Phoenix campus of Karsten Manufacturing, it is hard to imagine that this multimillion-dollar company started out in the most humble of surroundings: a family garage.

When Karsten moved from Redwood City to take a position in General Electric's Phoenix plant, he and Louise looked for a house with a big garage. They found it, and he again set up his club-making shop there. The club-making business was truly a family affair in the Solheim home. By this time it was just Karsten, Louise, and John, all deeply involved. John's siblings would all one day follow their father and brother into the business.

John, just starting in high school at the time of the move to Phoenix, continued to assemble clubs after school and on weekends while Karsten worked on club designs. Karsten enjoyed working with his youngest son. They had their difficulties working together, but it was a good arrangement, both because of the help John provided and because it gave him time with his father. It also was the beginning of John's learning the business, and that prepared him to take over at the top of Karsten Manufacturing many years later.

When John first started helping his father, he wasn't paid for his efforts. This was, after all, a family business, and family members should be expected to help out. That changed after the move to Paradise Valley. When a grocery store went up in the area—which, although a thriving area now, was sparsely populated back then—John, like many of his buddies in school, applied for a job. Karsten wasn't pleased, and he soon realized he would have to pay John in order to keep him from taking a job away from home. He did exactly that and set up an arrangement where John was paid a certain amount per putter.

A TOUGH DAD (AND BOSS) TO PLEASE

A sad fact of life is that success and wealth—sudden or not, deserved or not—do not make a better person. Some newly wealthy people are able to improve their lives; others are ruined. But all who experience a sudden increase in income find that this merely showcases who they really are.

The real Karsten Solheim, at the time of his boost into significant wealth, was a man maturing both spiritually and emotionally. He could still be stubborn and opinionated. He had a one-track mind. There was Karsten's way and the wrong way.

But, strangely, with the maturing of his own children and with their partnership in the business, he became a better father. Louise had already seen tremendous growth in him as a husband. He was more thoughtful and more sensitive. He loved people and was widely admired, respected, and even revered as a boss. He still wasn't perfect and never would be. But his old spiritual virtues, his love for God, his generosity, his sweetness and empathy for the less fortunate—these came to the fore as he aged.

But he could be impatient. He demanded quality and perseverance, and he would not abide shortcuts, shoddy work, or bargain buying at the expense of the final product. Again, as is so often the case, his strengths often were merely the other side of the coin from his weaknesses. Some saw him as an eccentric, others as a kook. The people who really knew him and loved him and either worked for him or lived with him, or both, accepted him warts and all and felt blessed to be influenced by him.

Karsten's sons are realistic about him. They recognize his genius, and they admire the huge operation he built from a simple idea. But they also admit that he was an inspiration and an encourager to any employee other than a family member. Somehow, each found it hard to please him, to satisfy him, to reach his standard. To some this was motivational, and they bear no pain from it. He was just being Karsten, they say. They grew to understand and appreciate him. Maybe they wished he would occasionally be as supportive of them as he was of other employees, but they have long since quit worrying about it.

Eventually all four Solheim children would move to Phoenix and work for the Karsten Manufacturing Corporation. John was more or less born into it, and Allan moved to Phoenix in 1962, where he worked nights at GE as a computer operator while working days for his father on the first irons. In 1963 he met and married Joan Chandler. In 1967, he left GE to work full-time for what was by then incorporated as Karsten Manufacturing.

Both John and Allan recall Karsten's still being a tough man to work for, even when it was a side business at home.

It was not unusual for their father to come home from

a long day at GE, watch the late evening news, then wake up John even on a school night and tell him it was time to work. They would build putters for an hour or so before John went back to bed. John felt put-upon at the time, but it was preparation he would one day need to become president of the company. Also, he says, "Some of those original putters are worth thousands today as collectors' items because of what the company has become."

Karsten was, for a fact, difficult to please, and that pickiness when it came to work became part of a now-legendary family story:

One day he told John to clean up the shop. John invested several hours in the project, including reorganizing all the tool drawers and cabinets. By the time he was finished, he was convinced his dad would be thrilled with the shipshape accessibility of everything. The only problem was that while he had spent all his time on stuff that was now hidden behind closed doors and in drawers, he had forgotten to straighten up the main workbench.

When Karsten came home from work and took a look at the garage, he exploded. He told John in no uncertain terms that it was time he found work somewhere else. He went so far as to get the newspaper, turn to the classifieds, and thrust it into John's hands. "You find where you want to apply, and I'll drop you there on my way to work tomorrow," he said.

John and Allan put their heads together and hatched a plan to get their father's attention. They were going to call his bluff. They decided what they would do, then confided in their mother so she wouldn't be alarmed at what was about to happen.

The next morning, Karsten demanded to know if John had made a decision and had a destination. John gave him the address of his would-be employer, and Karsten drove him downtown for what he thought was an interview for his son. Allan had agreed to pick up John after the interview.

A few minutes after dropping John off, Karsten returned home, obviously upset. Allan and Louise watched from the window as he made his way into the house. They had an idea of what was about to happen, but they kept their composure.

"You're not going to work?" she asked innocently.

"Later," Karsten said, then dropped the news: "Well, we've lost our son."

"What do you mean?" Louise asked, well knowing what her husband was talking about.

"The address he had me take him to was the army recruiter's office!"

Louise, always one to enjoy a good joke, fought to control herself. She couldn't laugh now, not with the payoff so close.

"It's your fault, you know," he said.

"*My* fault?" Louise said. It was almost too much for her to keep from laughing.

"You didn't make him follow through on what I told him to do! If you had seen to it that he cleaned the garage properly, this wouldn't have happened!"

"Well, did you sign anything?" she asked, knowing that John wasn't old enough to join the service without his parent's signature.

"Did I sign anything?"

"At the recruiter's office. The boy is seventeen years old. He's not going anywhere without his father's permission."

That cooled Karsten a bit, and he went off to work. Meanwhile, Allan went to pick up John.

When he got home, John stood around sheepishly, wondering what to do. He was, after all, still a kid, and he had no idea what he should do next.

He asked his mother, "What do you think I ought to do?"

Louise said, "Why don't you just finish cleaning the garage the way your dad told you?"

John did as she told him. He went to the garage and transformed it into a model of neatness and efficiency. He left no doubt in his mind that his father would be pleased.

When Karsten got home that evening, he found his son working in the sparkling garage. "Now *that's* the way I like it," he said, paying John something as close to a compliment as he ever paid him.

John, and later Allan and Louis, all learned the golf-club business "the way their father liked it," and from the perspective of forty years in the business, it was providential that the current chairman/CEO, John, and the executive vice president, Allan, learned the business from the ground up. When Karsten meandered around the huge complex and watched the hundreds of workers, they were doing what he did from the beginning. And when John runs a meeting or sets a budget or dreams up a new design, he's doing it with an entire adult life's worth of experience in making golf clubs virtually from scratch.

LOUISE'S STRUGGLE

After the move to Phoenix, Louise had no time to find other employment. She kept busy picking up supplies, writing orders, mailing clubs, and keeping the books for her husband's fledgling business. She was good at that kind of work, because in the summer of 1958 she had gone to work for Ampex. She was on the staff of the manager of manufacturing, and it seemed to her she was working on budgets all the time—sales budgets, production budgets, manpower budgets, cash-flow budgets. All that would prove excellent preparation for the future of the Karsten Manufacturing Corporation, which, of course, did not even exist yet.

Something was deeply troubling to Louise, besides the

fact that they had moved away from the rest of her beloved children. After graduating as an electrical engineer from the University of Wyoming, Louis would go to work for IBM in San Diego. Allan would go into sales for a California firm, and Sandra was working for *Sunset Magazine* in Menlo Park.

No, it was more than that. From the beginning there was something she had resented about the whole idea of a putter business. She was impressed that Karsten had come up with a brilliant idea and that it seemed to be catching on. She even thought it might make a nice retirement hobby and something to fall back on. But the very game of golf was something that kept people out of church on Sundays. It had even affected her deeply spiritual husband that way. He still loved God, and he ran his business dealings with an eye on biblical principles. He still attended church (though not as faithfully as before). But there was always a round to play, a tournament to get to or compete in, a sale to make, whether it was on a Sunday or not. That bothered her.

There was still something else that bothered her about this business. It occurred to her that she felt as if she had been drafted, that if it were her choice she wouldn't be doing the work she was doing. Karsten had never really said anything about her duties with the new company; they just more or less fell into her lap. She wasn't happy about it, either.

Once they had relocated to Phoenix, Karsten's main job was still at GE, of course. And John was off to high school every day. So who did that leave with all that had to be done to keep the new business afloat? Louise felt as if she had no choice. John helped manufacture the putters at night, and in Karsten's downtime he was out hustling up orders.

She was expected to fill those orders, ship those putters, invoice those customers, keep track of the income, and bank the money. Basically, she was running the business, this monster her genius husband had spawned.

There were days when Louise was so burdened by the work that she was tempted to throw all the paperwork into the fireplace. Orders and letters with money enclosed and invoices came in, and she had to do something with them. She knew that big trouble might come if records weren't kept.

Once she even approached their pastor and told him of her ill feelings about the business. It wasn't that Louise felt that she was overworked; it was that she couldn't reconcile being involved in the golf-club business as something pleasing to God. She thought about all those golfers who skipped church in favor of heading to the golf course. And that bothered her.

But even the pastor concluded, "Making golf clubs is a legitimate business." He asked her if money—striving for monetary wealth—was Karsten's motivation. "No," she said, "he seems to care little about money. Just keep the bills paid. Karsten strives for perfection in whatever he does and wants recognition for it. I believe that recognition is what motivates him."

Every day got worse. Louise dreaded the mail. She dreaded sitting down and processing everything. She endured for as long as she could, and when the temptation to burn the orders reached its zenith, she came to the end of herself. It was time to apply her deep, lifelong faith. If there was no other answer to her dilemma, surely she needed to turn it over to God. A sob rising in her throat, she made her way back to her bedroom and dropped to her knees.

"Lord," Louise prayed desperately, "help me. Either make this business go away, make people quit buying the putters, or make me willing to accept it."

She went back to work, feeling hollow. All she knew was that she had been sincere. If God blessed the business and made it even more prosperous, she just hoped He honored her request and allowed her to live with it. She couldn't stand resenting it so. And Karsten didn't even notice!

About a week later, Louise rose as usual and went to her "desk" (actually, it was the family breakfast table), when Karsten and John had left for the day. She busied herself with her work, finally pausing to realize, *I'm not minding this anymore. The Lord must be working and making me willing to accept this golf-club business.*

Karsten didn't like Louise to tell that story, but it was a critical point in the life of the Ping business. The putter business began to grow beyond all expectations, convincing Louise that God was involved in it. And that was critical because, as anyone who is familiar with the Ping business can attest, Louise Solheim has been absolutely crucial in getting and keeping the business running at the level it has.

Karsten many times referred to Louise as "my eyes and ears" and "my memory," and that was certainly apt. Louise is a perceptive woman with exceptional people skills. She has been, in fact, the strength where Karsten was weakest. But she has also been a catalyst for some ideas that have helped make Karsten's clubs the success they have been.

PERSUADING HIS FIRSTBORN

Karsten Louis, the Solheims' eldest son, was the last of the three sons to join Karsten Manufacturing, and he turned down his father's first offer to come to work for him. There was already tension between father and son because, before Karsten Manufacturing had incorporated, Karsten and Lou worked for competing computer companies, GE and IBM. The competition wasn't the problem; Lou sensed that Karsten would have preferred his son to work with him at GE.

Lou would work for IBM for twelve years. In 1970,

when Karsten first approached him about moving to Phoenix, Lou had just committed to a new assignment at IBM and felt he should honor that. It was hard for Karsten to argue with that, because he had always taught his children to honor their word. Lou was in a creative group in IBM's scientific research center, and he enjoyed it.

Later, Karsten asked him, as a computer expert, to evaluate the company's need for a computer and make a recommendation. Lou told him, "Dad, as an employee of IBM, all I could tell you was to buy IBM. What I will do, however, is come and evaluate your company and help you understand your own organization."

As Karsten Manufacturing was not large yet, Louis's evaluation took only a few days. He tracked the flow of information through Karsten's system and found it tight and efficient. He marveled anew at his father's ability to continually find ways to make things better.

Karsten was ahead of his time in practicing what management experts now call MBWA—Management By Walking Around. As Karsten had built the operation from the ground up, there wasn't a task in any stage of the operation that he couldn't perform. He was able to visualize how a step could be improved, could sit at a desk or work on the line for a few minutes, and go formulate a solution. Of his many gifts, that ability was one of the most profound.

Karsten's hands-on approach and quick thinking almost made a computer unnecessary at first. Lou charted the organization and told his father he should simply show the chart to whatever computer company he was considering and find out which of the steps on the chart it could streamline for him.

Lou says, "His system was so efficient already that it was hard to break through it and make a computer help. Most of the salespeople he talked to resorted to simply selling the benefits of their computers without really knowing what they were talking about."

His son's help made Lou only more attractive to Karsten Manufacturing, but it would be five more years before he could be persuaded to join the firm. If Lou had waited until his father's venture became an acknowledged success before he gave up his own blossoming career with IBM, who could blame him? But perhaps Karsten retained some resentment regarding the delay.

Lou believes that one of the best lessons he ever learned from his father came at the chessboard. Karsten used to warn him, when Lou was younger, "Don't make that play, or I'll do this. Don't do this, or I'll do that."

From that Lou learned to look ahead, become analytical, think of consequences. When he joined the company, his father admitted he had not really thought through a job description. He merely knew he needed a thinker like Lou on the team, and he began assigning him tasks that seemed not to fall within anyone else's parameters of responsibility.

Lou at first worried about working for a father he had always seen as spare with encouragement and compliments. The first time he had ever beaten Karsten in chess, his father mentioned "good game" in passing the next day, and Lou realized that was as close to praise as he had ever received. It remains a highlight of Lou's relationship with him.

Lou came to realize that one positive result of his rather formal relationship with his father was that he had learned to stay at various tasks without living and dying for praise or even attention. There was some benefit in that, which was confirmed for him every time he saw an employee who seemed starved for one kind word from the boss.

One of Lou's first tasks was to rearrange the front office so that customer service could have some privacy during the workday. He tried two rearrangements of the desks, which met with some complaining, then found a solution everyone seemed pleased with. He made the change, and the next day overheard Karsten tell someone else, "This is nice, isn't it?"

The irony, of course, was that Karsten seemed generous with praise and acceptance and encouragement for those workers who were not related to him.

LOUISE'S ANS(W)ER

Karsten was still working for GE in 1963 while the home business was beginning to expand and the rest of the family was also in transition. Allan married Joan Chandler. Louise took a seminar in foreign trade at Arizona State University.

Previous to that, a letter had come from Johannesburg, South Africa, ordering a putter like the one Allan Henning was using. Louise went to the United States Department of Commerce in Phoenix to inquire what procedures were needed to sell internationally. It sounded so complicated that she decided just to send two putters as a gift.

In the fall of 1964, high school grad John tried college away from home. For a half year, he attended LeTourneau College in Texas, a Christian college specializing in engineering and manufacturing technology, before coming back to stay at Karsten's side, enroll at Arizona State University, and live at home. It would be his only absence from the business since its inception.

As the business grew, Louise came to a point where she realized that there was just too much work for her to do alone. She hired a neighbor, Polly Hogg, to assist in doing the record keeping. Polly became the first person of thousands of people outside the family to work in the business. The card system of cross-checking work in progress that she and Louise set up would serve the company for the next eight or nine years.

Karsten traveled a lot in those days to follow the PGA Tour. He had decided to sell only through golf pros and to build clubs only by order. Jim Hansberger, who would later become president of Ram Golf, was a friendly competitor whose travels often coincided with Karsten's. Many years later, Hansberger remembered those trips fondly, recounting Karsten's persistence in selling the tour players on his ugly but functional putter.

Karsten refused to mass market his clubs or to sell them to discount or department stores. When Sears Roebuck sent a request on pricing for several hundred putters on a regular basis, he refused to consider it. That early decision to make Ping clubs available only by special order led to a demand for them that was unprecedented.

A golfer had to really want a Ping putter. He couldn't just go in and buy it off the rack. He had to custom-order it (putters were not as precisely measured as the irons were), be measured for it, and pay top dollar for it. The Ping became a prestigious club to own. It was a statement.

Ironically, the more successful the home-based putter business became, the less time Karsten had for playing golf or bowling. Neither he nor Louise had much experience in business, yet he made the strategy calls and did remarkably well. Ever driven to improve on what he had done before, he continued to design new putters and by the end of 1965 had designed a total of twenty-one models. His most successful putter was yet to come.

When Karsten came home from the Los Angeles Open in January of 1966, he complained that it seemed everyone was playing with an Arnold Palmer putter. "I've got to find an answer to it."

Right away he started developing a design he believed would be an answer to Palmer's club. He went to work on a blueprint of sorts—actually it was a drawing on the sleeve of an old 78 rpm record, which was found recently in Louise's office. He came up with a brilliant new idea and fashioned a heel-toe balanced putter with a gooseneck hosel.

When the new putter was ready for engraving, Karsten asked Louise, "What shall we call it?"

"Call it 'the Answer,'" she said, remembering that he had designed the putter as an answer to the Arnold Palmer models.

"What kind of name is that?" he asked. "That's no name for a putter."

They didn't discuss the name of the putter further that day, but when it was time to take the putter to the engraver the next morning, he still hadn't thought of a name. Again he asked her for a suggestion.

"I have to take this putter to the engraver today," he said. "What shall we call it?"

"Call it the Answer," she repeated.

There was a slight problem with naming the club the Answer, and Karsten knew what it was. The word *Answer* was too long to fit on the toe of the putter—at least in letters large enough to be easily seen. In order for it to fit, the club head would have to be bigger, and that would totally change its design. "PING" fit nicely on the heel. But he had experimented with "Answer," and no matter what he did, it didn't look right. It was just too small to be seen. He'd eventually given up on using the word, exasperated that Louise had even suggested it to him.

"It's too long of a word," Karsten said. "It won't fit."

"Is *that* the problem?" Louise then quickly suggested that they spell "Answer" as it sounds. She said, "It should fit nicely if you leave out the 'W.'"

Karsten either liked the idea, or he was in too much of a hurry to wait for another one. After all, he had already had success with the name "Ping," so another funny name couldn't hurt. He took the club to the engravers, had "Anser" engraved on it, then introduced his Scottsdale Anser putter in February of 1966.

A BIG SUCCESS

The Anser putter was an overwhelming success. Sales went through the roof almost immediately. By October 1966, they would be so good that the Solheims would have to move the business out of their home and to a new facility in northwest Phoenix. The demand for the Anser continues to this day. It is among the best-selling putters—if not *the* best-selling—in the history of golf. In February 1999, it received the "Putter of the Year" award in Great Britain.

Karsten's recognizing that Louise had a good idea—the name "Anser"—was a major step in their relationship and his personal growth, too. It was also a huge moment in the history of Ping golf clubs. Although his initial reaction had been typical Karsten (wanting all ideas to be his own), her suggestion for a slight change sounded right to him, and he was big enough to admit it.

That was a small foundation to build on, especially for a man in his midfifties, but as he slowly grew to the point where he listened to Louise and then began to seek her input and advice, he found her a tremendous resource. Many point to Louise's quiet savvy as one of the backbones of the immensely successful industry Ping has become.

That savvy, that seemingly inborn insight, that made Louise so important in the Ping business, would be vital later. There was something big coming for Karsten and Ping golf clubs—his biggest step to that point in getting his business going—that Louise would have a major say in. And it wouldn't be long after the introduction of the Anser that Karsten would again accept the wise counsel of his wife.

12

MAKING STRIDES

The Start of Karsten Manufacturing

Just about anyone who has accomplished anything great in any arena of life has had to take risks. Karsten Solheim was no exception.

Nineteen sixty-six had been a pivotal year for Ping golf clubs. Karsten introduced the Anser putter, and it was met with instant acceptance among professional and amateur golfers alike. It seemed that everybody who saw the Anser or tried it out wanted one for his or her own golf bag. The reason was simple: It worked. Its heel-toe-weighted design, the introduction of a hosel with bends in it (giving the club more stability), as well as other technological advances had made the Anser everything Karsten had hoped it would be. It may have looked different—strange in most people's eyes—but players loved the way it performed.

It soon became obvious that the little golf-club company had outgrown the family garage. Karsten had to find a more suitable place to operate his business. Soon they would move to the original Karsten Manufacturing building at 21st Avenue and Desert Cove Avenue, on the property where their entire conglomerate stands today. They use that 2,200-square-foot building now as a club repair shop.

BRINGING SANDRA HOME

Karsten and Louise persuaded daughter Sandra to join the new company as a receptionist. She had moved so many times with the family that she had enjoyed putting down roots in California. But she also liked the idea of rejoining her family, so she came to Phoenix and has worked for the company ever since.

Louise was proud of Sandra for having lived on her own for several years. She proved popular as the first receptionist in the new building because of her sweet spirit and her love of meeting new people. People who met her in her earlier years at Karsten Manufacturing still remember her when she was the receptionist.

Louise went to Palo Alto to help Sandra move to Phoenix. It happened that the 1966 U.S. Open was about to be held at the Olympic Club in San Francisco, and, of course, Karsten wanted her to see the golf pro there to try to promote the putters. Louise agreed to stop at the Olympic Club to present the putters.

As usual, she felt totally out of her element when she visited the club, but when she walked in the door and the pro came to meet her, she would have a new experience.

"Where can I get more of these putters?" he asked. "Every player here has one in his bag."

She assured him they could supply them. At that point, Louise knew beyond any doubt that the putters were going to be a big success.

They were a big success, and they got to be a success with a little help, and some timely breaks, along the way.

GOING BIG TIME

Bob Goetz was the first touring pro to use the Ping putter on tour. He later was the pro at the Longview Country Club in Longview, Texas, near where John attended college. When John needed spending money, he would sell Goetz a couple of the putters he had brought with him from home. Babe Hiskey, one of the first pros to represent the company and who still plays on the senior tour and represents Ping, took a supply of putters on the tour with him and talked other golfers into trying them. He sold them into the pro shops, too.

Karsten also got great help from Rocky Thompson, another current senior tour player. Thompson took the putters to different tour stops and gave players a chance to try them out. He is credited with getting high-profile players such as Jack Nicklaus, Gary Player, Gene Littler, and George Archer to use the putter.

The business got a significant shot in the arm from the Canada Cup, now called the World Cup, which was held in Tokyo in 1966. At that time, the big three of golf were Arnold Palmer, Jack Nicklaus, and Gary Player. Nicklaus, playing for the United States, used a Ping Cushin putter, as did Player, who played for South Africa, used an Anser. They joined pros such as Julius Boros, Doug Sanders, and Chi Chi Rodriguez in using Ping putters. Suddenly, leading pros such as Jack Nicklaus and Gary Player wanted licenses to sell Pings internationally.

Ping had, for a fact, gone major league.

The putter's distinctive look showed well on television, and soon it seemed everyone wanted one. Louise and Karsten received phone calls in the wee hours of the morning from people all around the world—many speaking very broken English in thick accents—wanting to know how to get Ping putters. There was an avalanche of orders. Karsten's putters were becoming the rule rather than the exception in many tournaments.

With all that success, some people, including Louise, wondered when Karsten would begin working full-time to manufacture and sell his clubs.

ONE HUGE DECISION

When Karsten began designing, manufacturing, and selling his putters, he received some very sound advice, which he wisely took: "Don't quit your day job." So he continued to work for General Electric after he decided to start marketing the clubs, even during the time when tour pros began using them and during the time he was designing the Anser. Even when the putters began catching on in 1966, he never intended to leave his job at GE, opting to make the putters a side business while he kept his security and his pension with his employer.

Louise, on the other hand, had been keeping the company's books, and she knew that Ping had become something more than a side business. She knew they were selling more than enough putters to make a living, a good living.

Many people, including Karsten's parents, thought it would be unwise of him to quit at GE and rely on this sideline business of his. After all, he had fourteen years in with the company. He had job security, great pay, a great retirement plan. Karsten gave it some thought, but Louise got to a point where she didn't have to think about it anymore. She knew it was the thing to do. She was confident that the business was going to be an enormous success, and, as much as she didn't like contradicting Karsten's parents, she decided to strongly encourage him to leave GE. She could see that the timing was right for him to make golf clubs his full-time occupation.

GE was aware of Karsten's success in his side business, and, in an attempt to keep him, they offered him positions in a variety of interesting locations. He checked out all of them, but Louise still urged him to resign.

One day, Karsten came home from work and announced that GE wanted to transfer him and the plant he worked at in Phoenix to Oklahoma City. Neither he nor Louise wanted to move to Oklahoma City. He interviewed for a job with GE at the Space Center and was preparing to move to Daytona Beach when Gus Grissom and two other astronauts died in the fire that broke out in their craft during a ground test. At that point, Karsten decided he would never work in the space industry. He also visited a GE plant in Boston but thought the climate there was too cold.

All this got Karsten to thinking that maybe Louise was right. Maybe it was time to throw himself into the golf-club business, time to make that his primary occupation.

In January 1967, Karsten made his decision and left GE. They generously gave him a severance package of a week's salary for each of the fourteen years he had worked there. The Solheims were on their own now and soon had fifteen employees. They incorporated that midyear, and the Karsten Manufacturing Corporation was officially born.

They were flush with what appeared an overnight success, but if they thought business was booming then, they had a surprise coming just a few months later.

KARSTEN MANUFACTURING

When Karsten Manufacturing incorporated in 1967, John left Arizona State University to help train the company's first fifteen employees. Karsten thought he had it made, arranging the layout of his little 2,200-square-foot building with desks in the front and production in the back. Karsten Manufacturing is now housed in thirty-plus buildings at its expanded location.

If there was one big break for Ping in 1967, it came when forty-six-year-old Julius Boros, a pro who had been putting poorly, switched to a Ping putter and won the Phoenix Open. That made him the first to win a PGA Tour event with one of Karsten's putters, a Cushin model that Boros has said was the ugliest putter ever invented. (Karsten used the spellings "Cushin" and "Kushin" for different models.)

John Barnum was the first golfer to win a professional tournament with a Ping B69 putter (a putter the pros nicknamed the "hot dog," both from its shape and its performance), taking a senior win about 1962. The Ping club showed well on television, and anyone who had not already heard of the new phenomenon was aware of it now. For decades, Ping putters would dominate the market.

A BIG TRIP

About that time, Karsten and Louise planned a three-week trip to investigate world markets. It would be the first time they would spend that much time alone together in more than thirty years of marriage. The plan was to visit England to talk about licensing with Japan because they already did so much business there, and because the contract with Jack Nicklaus had to include them, and Norway so that Karsten could visit the land of his birth for the first time since coming to America. Then Karsten's travel agent informed him that, because his original ticket took him to those three countries, he could travel anywhere in the world for the same price. Suddenly the trip became a monster as Karsten and Louise added stops all over the globe and seven more weeks to the journey.

Karsten, who loved meeting people and welcoming visitors to his new plant, looked forward to the international trip. For her part, Louise confided to friends that she doubted he had the patience for a three-week trip and would be eager to get home and back to work as quickly as possible. She had underestimated him, though, as he had underestimated her for so many years.

The Solheims left on July 4 and were gone ten weeks. They attended the British Open and then visited Norway, Switzerland, Greece, India, Thailand, Hong Kong, Japan, and Alaska. They didn't get home to Phoenix until after Labor Day.

Louise, with her love of travel, enjoyed every minute of it, especially seeing Karsten get acquainted with relatives in Norway he had never met. He considered no one a stranger. They visited the island where his mother was born and raised and where his grandfather had been active in the local church. His grandfather's picture was on the wall of the church's mission room.

When the Solheims asked to meet anyone from the Koppen family, they were directed to the homes of several relatives. They welcomed Karsten and Louise as long-lost loved ones, and each wanted to give them something as a memento of the trip.

Karsten and Louise saw the tiny home where Karsten's father was born. It now belonged to cousins who had never seen Louise, yet there on the wall was a photograph of her and the children. When they ferried back to the mainland at the end of the day, all the relatives saw them off and waved white hankies in farewell.

In Bangkok, Karsten had to ask where a golf course was. When he located it, he tried to sell putters to the pro, who showed little interest. But something happened during the night to change the pro's mind. The next morning he awakened the Solheims by banging on their hotel room door and begged to place an order. He had talked to some local golfers who informed him that Ping putters were the hottest items in the world. To order directly from the designer and manufacturer was a privilege he didn't want to miss.

Karsten said later in a speech that he wasn't sure how he was going to feel being with Louise day after day, all night and all day for that long. He added simply, "It was a wonderful trip." It was the highest compliment he had ever paid her.

Indeed, they seemed to bond on that tour. He found her to be a gracious diplomat, articulate, good-natured, humorous, and also full of ideas. His quiet and generous friendliness was not a surprise to her, but, though his busyness and his innovative brilliance were legendary, she was nearly overwhelmed at how he kept playing one new thought off another. She had recognized his genius early, yet the decades of family pressures, the tension over what she felt was his lack of spending enough time with the children, the building of a new business—all these contributed to her nearly forgetting about his astoundingly creative mind.

They talked. They shared. They laughed. He was still Karsten, knowing what he wanted, often wanting to make changes in schedule to work something else in. But he was also patient and friendly, especially with strangers, and that made Louise wish he had always been that way with those who loved him most.

She knew he would prove to be a kindly and usually patient boss, and that employees would love to have him greet them and be able to call him by his first name. But she was a little skittish about having their children join the company. It seemed ironic that he had had little time for them while they were growing up, yet now he wanted them around him in the business. She didn't know if it would work. Of course, it did.

Louise was most encouraged upon their return, because Karsten seemed to have even a new spiritual temperature. He seemed to look at her and appreciate her in a new light. She always wanted to be his helpmate and companion by supporting him in whatever he did. She was glad that others had been hired to handle the money and the orders. She was more fulfilled with the freedom to travel, to be one he could bounce ideas off, and to strategize marketing and sales. Her training came in handy, and although she didn't see herself as a creative-idea person, she came to be known as a good reactor. She could hear an idea and see its strengths and weaknesses. She could envision where it might lead. Plus, she was so articulate and nurturing that everyone loved her.

Karsten and Louise spent much of their time back then traveling to promote their product. There was hardly a time when they weren't somewhere in the country or overseas at tour events. The results were remarkable. Sales of the putters skyrocketed, going from $50,000 in sales in 1966 to $800,000 in 1968—a 1,500 percent increase in just two years!

Later, Louise would tell how the familiar company logo came into being about the time of their world trip:

> Karsten and I were about to leave on our first overseas trip together. The date was early July 1967. The luggage was in the car, the tickets were in our hands, and we walked together into John's office to tell him we were ready to go. Karsten spotted a strange looking little clay figure on John's desk. "What is that?" he asked John.
>
> "Oh, I was just doodling with the modeling clay," was John's reply.
>
> The little figure of a short, stout man with a hat on and a putter in his hand ready to putt seemed to fascinate Karsten. "I like it. Don't destroy it!" he said. "I want to see it when I get back." A plane was waiting, there was no time to linger. The trip would take us around the world visiting markets and possible markets. We would not return home for ten weeks, arriving just after Labor Day.
>
> On our way home, the little clay man, whom we

dubbed Pingman, was intact, but we were surprised to find in front of the offices a two-and-a-half-foot replica made of wire and plaster of paris by Allan and artist Jan Gargero. Jan, Allan's sister-in-law, was visiting at the time. Shortly after our arrival home, it was decided to use Pingman as our company logo, and an application for a trademark was filed.

Things were going well for Karsten, but he wasn't about to sit on his laurels and enjoy his success. All that time he was designing and planning, looking ahead to a time when he would make history with another invention: the best-selling iron of all time.

A TIME OF EXPANSION

It might be tempting to think that Karsten's idea to get into the iron business came only after the putters caught on. But that was not the way it happened. He had thought about building a matched set of irons from the beginning.

In the early '60s, he made several trips to Fernquist and Johnson, a Bay area wholesale golf-club maker, to look into iron design. Irons at this time were all forged. They would be purchased in rough form and individually placed in a powerful press, which would come down with thousands of pounds of pressure to stamp the shape and design on each iron head. It was a noisy and messy process, and it did not lend itself to the custom work Karsten was thinking about.

He had come up with an idea for iron design that was as innovative as his initial heel-and-toe weighting for the putter. He theorized that perimeter weighting—in other words, a rim of extra metal around the outside of the back of an iron blade—would make an iron more stable and allow it to strike the ball squarer, driving it straighter and farther.

Shortly after the family (reduced in size to Karsten, Louise, and John) moved to Phoenix, Karsten and Louise drove to Escondido to visit the Golfcraft factory, which was headed by Ted Woolley, a much respected Scottish golf-club designer and manufacturer. They sat with him in his office while Karsten explained his theories of an innovative iron design.

Mr. Woolley listened quietly but with interest. It was obvious that Karsten's ideas would require considerable handwork. He asked a few questions, thought for a moment, then said, "I'll tell you what I'll do. I'm going to let you have a hundred sets of iron-head blanks. You take them home and do whatever you're going to do, then send them back to us, and we'll chrome-plate them, returning the finished heads to you to shaft and grip."

Karsten was elated. From that day on, he never stopped expressing his gratitude and appreciation for Ted Woolley's early assistance.

Karsten put the ten burlap bags of iron-head blanks in the trunk of his 1959 Citroen (that car was his pride and joy back then). As soon as he got back to Phoenix, he called Allan in Palo Alto. Allan had returned from a six-month Marines Reserves duty and was selling Cutco Cutlery, then a Wearever product sold at home parties. Karsten asked Allan if he could come to Phoenix for a couple of months to help him do the milling of the iron heads.

Allan said he would and arrived soon, accompanied by a little white kitten, which he gave to Louise. He said one of his customers told him she would buy some of the cutlery if he would take one of her kittens. Louise told him the kitten should be named "Down Payment," but that was too long, so they settled on "Cutco."

To get the weight distribution Karsten believed an iron should have to improve performance, he knew he would have to remove weight from the middle of the iron head. To accomplish this, he milled out two elliptical cavities in the back of each club head, keeping in mind the desired finished weight needed for each iron in a set. To weigh the heads, Karsten had rigged up a water-displacement system using a bucket of water on the floor and an iron head on a little tray attached to a pulley, which he lowered into the bucket.

As he got some of the sets finished, he would try them out himself and persuade others to try them, also. These first irons were called the 69 Model. He named it 69, because that is a good golf score. Some came out in late 1961.

Babe Hiskey, Joel Goldstrand, Rocky Thompson, and Ken Fulton were some of the pros Karsten persuaded to try those first experimental irons with the hand-milled cavity backs. Over the next three or four years, he got about three hundred sets from Golfcraft or Fernquist & Johnson.

Another model of experimental clubs, which came out in 1966 and was still forged, had just one large cavity in the back and was called the "Anser" Model. They were still hand milled, hand weighted, but with an innovation in the grip added. What Karsten called the "Ballnamic" grip had a very slight bend near the top of the shaft. The bend stabilized the club during the swing. He obtained a patent on it. Sales on these irons improved all the time, but production was slow because of all the handwork.

Karsten chrome plated the early irons. He later found that by investment casting the heads he could eliminate the glare from the chrome. Instead, the stainless steel heads were tumbled in a large tumbling machine, which gave them a pewter look for a finish. They looked strange, and they were the most expensive on the market. People couldn't buy them except through a local golf pro. They were also the best on the market and remained the most popular.

One golf club in the eastern United States ordered more than forty sets in a year's time. Karsten phoned the pro, Bud Timbrook, and thanked him for the orders and said how much he appreciated the interest in Ping irons.

"Well," said Timbrook, "the handicaps of the members who had bought Ping have dropped dramatically, and everyone wants to get in on the act."

It looked as if Karsten's irons might be met with the same enthusiastic acceptance as the putters had. But a big setback on both putter and irons was ahead.

In the spring of 1967, the United States Golf Association (USGA), the all-powerful rule maker of golf in the United States, announced that the rules for golf-club specifications would now include a stipulation that there could be no bend in the shaft more than five inches above the sole of the club. This meant that Karsten's patented Ballnamic bend under the grip was now nonconforming, and several of the putter models that had the "Big Z" bend just above the hosel were also affected. Fortunately, the best-selling Anser putter was *not* affected.

This major setback came just weeks after Karsten had left his position at GE, hired fifteen additional full-time employees, and had finally agreed to let several persistent salesmen sell Ping putters. The three or four touring professionals using Ping irons made frantic phone calls to Karsten for advice. They had been told they couldn't use the irons, so they had to obtain other equipment. Karsten appreciated their dilemma, but he had no immediate answer. It was back to the drawing board.

This was also a time when the Solheim family drew together in prayer for their business. Karsten called the family into the company's office and explained to them that the USGA ruling had rendered a great many of their putters and irons illegal or, as it was worded by the USGA, "nonconforming." He told them, "I think we should pray about this," and he did. He prayed that if it was God's will for the business to continue, that He would cause them to prosper, but if it was His will for it to end, that they would accept that and be ready to move on. With that, Karsten went about doing what needed to be done for the company to survive this setback. For the next two years, roaring putter sales kept the newly incorporated company in business.

MORE DESIGNS

In December 1969, Karsten introduced the Karsten I iron, his first investment-cast club. Investment casting is a process in which a wax replica, an exact copy, is made of the part to be cast, then coated with ceramic or another heat-resistant material. After the outer coating hardens, the mold is heated so that the wax melts, leaving a hollow mold. Molten metal is then poured into the mold. The metal cools, and the mold is broken, leaving a perfect golf-club head. This process of investment casting ensured uniformity and accuracy in the clubs and eliminated the need for grinding them, which had to be done with forged clubs. Karsten had checked the irons of many pro players and found that many sets included more than one iron of the same loft. In other words, a set could have in reality included three or four 5 irons, even though only one of the clubs was stamped with a 5.

It didn't take long for other golf-club manufacturers to start using investment casting. Since then, almost all of them have gone to that process.

As he had with his putters, Karsten used an innovative design with the Karsten I iron, including perimeter weighting, heel-toe balance, and an offset hosel. Today, most manufacturers produce heel-toe-weighted putters and perimeter-weighted irons. Nothing else compares to the advantages those features give a golfer. Karsten always believed he could keep improving on his designs, and that became the only way to stay ahead of the competition. The Karsten II, III, and IV models soon followed the introduction of the Karsten I.

In 1979, he introduced the Ping Eye iron, another instant success, and in 1982, he followed that with the Eye2, the most popular iron ever created. More sets of the Eye2 have been sold than any other iron, and they are still selling strong today.

It was during this era that Karsten's custom fitting for clubs became a big hit. He had designed and copyrighted a color-coded fitting chart that allowed a golfer to purchase a set of clubs that was right for his or her height, hand size, and arm length. The design also enabled the club to be adjusted. He even taught his salesman to teach club pros to custom-fit for their customers. It was a revolutionary idea at the time, an idea that caught on in the rest of the industry.

STILL GOING STRONG

Amazingly, the newly incorporated business suffered little or no setback from the USGA. Putter sales kept soaring, Karsten and Louise left for their ten-week world-marketing trip, and it already was evident that their 2,200-square-foot workplace was inadequate. They needed more space and more workers. It wasn't long before Karsten Manufacturing began buying adjacent buildings and eventually building new ones. That expansion continued for several years. What had started as a small putter business grew to one that included putters, irons, woods, golf bags, golf balls, and other golf paraphernalia.

Over the years, the company would grow and grow, trying to keep up with demand. As many as 2,000 workers at one time populated Karsten Manufacturing, and even though the clubs had to be custom-made and no club was finished that had not been ordered, the factory was humming along at thousands of clubs a day. Karsten never released actual figures, since the company was a closely held corporation.

Because Karsten Manufacturing has always been privately owned, Karsten never had to release his financial information, either. Budgets, costs, profits, margins—nothing has ever been made public. *Forbes* magazine once estimated Karsten's personal fortune at $400,000,000. When members of the press were bold enough to ask how close was the *Forbes* estimate, Karsten merely smiled. Many believe he was implying that the estimate was far too generous. Others believe the opposite.

Karsten spent a lot of time developing the fitting chart that matches shaft length, club-head angle, and grip size to the size and shape and swing of each golfer. It is a color-coded system much simpler than it first appears. Golf club pros are taught to do the measuring and ordering, so that each customer gets a set of clubs color-coded to match his particular need. If his size or swing or anything else changes, Karsten Manufacturing is able to adjust his clubs.

Karsten's decision to turn down orders from such huge outlets as Sears had been controversial, even inside his own company. It's hard to turn down megaorders, and yet he always believed that his unique clubs would quickly get lost or be considered just "more equipment" if he didn't maintain exclusivity through the pro shops. That the clubs largely remain hard to get is part of the mystique, part of the attraction.

More than that, though, the clubs are in demand because they are a quality product that performs the way it was designed to. Karsten wouldn't have it any other way.

13

A NEAR TRAGEDY

Surviving Disaster in India

One of Karsten and Louise's early trips—in 1971, a mere four years after the company incorporated—turned out to be the couple's most memorable, both because of the variety of places they visited and because they were seriously injured and could have lost their lives in an automobile accident.

The trip was scheduled for three-and-a-half months, starting the first of July, and was to include stops in Spain, England, Denmark, Sweden, Norway, Finland, Russia, Poland, Czechoslovakia, Austria, Switzerland, Italy, Greece, Turkey, Israel, Kenya, Rhodesia, South Africa, India, Burma, Thailand, Singapore, and finally Australia, New Zealand, and Tahiti. It was part business, part pleasure, including a photographic safari in Kenya. The trip still holds vivid memories for Louise, and it also proved to be something of a landmark in John Solheim's life.

ANOTHER HOPE DEFERRED

Louise had suggested to youngest son John in 1967, when the company first started hiring women, that he should never date an employee. "You can't be a good supervisor if you've been out with them the night before," she told him, and he agreed.

Fast-forward four years to 1971. One morning, she could tell that John was nervous about something. He walked into the living room, then the family room, then back again.

"Have you got something on your mind, John?" she asked.

"Yes," he responded.

"Well, let's talk about it."

"I'm going to break one of your little rules," he said.

"Oh? Which one?"

"You know which one."

Indeed, Louise knew. He hadn't actually dated the girl yet, but she had seen Rhonda on his boat with other employees, and there seemed to be some chemistry between the two.

"Well," Louise cautioned, "as long as you know what you're doing."

"I do," he said prophetically.

Not long after, John came to Louise to tell her he and Rhonda were engaged. Louise asked if they would put off the marriage until she and Karsten returned from their world trip. So John and Rhonda's wedding was scheduled for ten days after their return, giving Louise little time for lists, invitations, and preparations. The fact that they returned even close to schedule proved to be just short of miraculous.

During the trip, they made business contacts and visited friends and missionaries. Seeing the missionaries in their homes and witnessing their work firsthand was inspiring and unforgettable. For both Louise and Karsten, that was the highlight of the trip.

The lowlight, however, resulted from their going to visit some missionary friends in Rewa, India.

ONE TOUGH DAY

Karsten and Louise had seen friends in Bombay and then flew to New Delhi, but monsoons made it impossible to stay on their air itinerary. Once settled in a hotel, they were determined to somehow get to Rewa. They were able to get as far as Agra and then Allahabad, where missionaries introduced them to an Indian convert who had taken the Christian name Timothy. He told them there were two ways to get to Rewa, about a hundred miles south of Allahabad, if they could cross the Ganges River.

Because of the heavy rains, no auto traffic was allowed on the bridge over the Ganges, and a train that would take them the long way around would add ten hours to their journey. Timothy suggested they walk across the bridge and then take a bus to Rewa.

The crazy Americans and Timothy were a sight, hiking across the nearly washed-out bridge, with a few nationals carrying most of their baggage and others just staring. But they found the bus to Rewa, made the trip, and spent three days there. The bus for the journey back to Allahabad never came, however. Timothy offered to get them a ride and located a Jeep, with driver and mechanic, for just $25. Karsten and Louise were both skeptical about the reliability and safety of this approach, but at that point they had little choice.

The Jeep was open, with cutout doors, but it looked serviceable enough. Karsten was initially jammed between Timothy and the mechanic on a bench in the back, while Louise sat in the front passenger seat. The ride was so bumpy, however, that Karsten soon left his big canvas bag of cameras, lenses, and film in the back, held onto his movie camera, and climbed up front between Louise and the driver.

From the beginning, it was clear that the driver had little experience. He drove too fast for the muddy roads, and even when he came to a long stretch of fresh gravel, he didn't back off on the gas. Louise had a bad feeling that something was going to happen. She hung on for dear life as Karsten tried to keep from bouncing first into the driver's lap and then into hers, all the while gripping his movie camera.

They came flying up to a narrow bridge, and Louise wondered how the driver would ever maneuver the bouncing vehicle over it. As he swerved first one way and then the other, trying to line up to cross over, he lost control. The Jeep fishtailed, straightened, skidded, then slid. They were careening toward the concrete bridge abutment, and still the driver didn't take his foot off the accelerator.

The Jeep smashed head-on into the abutment. The concrete was not steel reinforced, or all in the vehicle would have been killed. Instead, the Jeep sheared off the whole side of the bridge and was launched into the air. The first impact so viciously bounced the passengers that Karsten's movie camera smacked him in the chin and sliced a gash to the bone. Louise was struck in the back of the head by Karsten's canvas bag of cameras, and she saw stars. She watched in horror as the Jeep nose-dived toward a grassy embankment.

IS THIS IT?

In the split second before the vehicle hit the ground, Louise wondered, *Is this where my life is going to end, clear out here in India? I'm not even a missionary!*

At impact, Karsten and Louise were thrown out, flying at least twenty feet before slamming to the ground. Louise's arm had caught on something as she sailed out and tore a huge hole in her flesh. Timothy, who somehow stayed in the Jeep, hit his head on the roll bar and nearly scalped himself.

Louise landed on her side and felt as if her eyes had been pushed from their sockets. Her face was numb and would stay that way for a month. Karsten fell fully atop her before rolling off. His chin laceration was his only wound, but Louise felt mangled. She bled from her arm and her legs.

She watched as the Jeep rolled down into the water and Timothy and the driver scrambled out. She decided the mechanic had been thrown clear, too. The driver ran off, never to be seen by them again. Timothy staggered up toward Karsten and Louise, his head ripped open; it eventually required two hundred stitches.

Timothy found his overnight bag and pulled out a towel, which he wrapped around his head. He and Karsten approached Louise, asking if she was all right.

She wasn't, and she knew it. "I'm bleeding," she said, and already she felt pain all over her body, except in her numb face.

On the road above them, the men heard a vehicle. "Can you get up to the road with our help?" Karsten asked.

"I'll try," she said. "But where are my glasses?" She would be virtually helpless without them.

She spotted them nearby, but as she crawled to them and squinted, it appeared they were in pieces. When she reached for them, she realized Karsten's glasses had fallen right atop hers and they were wedged together, unharmed. Later, Allan's wife, Joan, would remark that "it was like the signature of your guardian angel."

Somehow they were able to get Louise up to the road in time to flag down the same bus heading toward Rewa that they had taken three days before. Looking as if they had been through a war, the three boarded for the ride back to Rewa, where they were delivered to Mahatma Gandhi Memorial Hospital. All Louise wanted was to get out of her bloody clothes and get treated.

She was to find that was not as simple a request as she thought.

A HOSPITAL IN NEED

Louise was nearly beside herself by the time the emergency staff began treating her most obvious wounds. "Get these bloody clothes off me!" she pleaded, but they continued to work on her. Karsten was somewhere on the phone, trying to get help from the U.S. embassy. Like Louise, his primary goal was to get her patched together enough to get out of the country and back to the States.

Louise again insisted they remove her bloody clothes, but they asked, "Do you have anything else to wear?"

Of course she hadn't. Most of their baggage was in New Delhi, and she had no idea what had become of the few things they had brought with them for the short stay in Rewa. It turned out they had been delivered to the hospital with them.

"Just put a hospital gown on me," Louise suggested.

That's when she was informed that this hospital was not like a stateside facility. All that was provided here were medical care and a bed. Everything else—from bedclothes to toiletries to toilet paper, soap, towels, even food—was to be provided by the patient.

X rays showed that Louise had a broken nose and a badly damaged left arm. The rest of her wounds were deep bruises, scrapes, and cuts, but she felt as if her entire body had been thrown out of kilter. Muscle and bone were visible through the huge hole in her arm, on which the staff concentrated most. The mashed flesh surrounding the wound was cut away and the wound dressed, but she was advised to have plastic surgery on it later.

Soon the Solheims' missionary friends arrived with all the supplies she would need. They said the bus driver had told them where she was.

"How did he know we knew you?" Louise asked.

"You're an American," they said, smiling. "He just assumed."

Their itinerary called for another month abroad, but all the Solheims wanted was to get home, where Louise could get the best care. The American ambassador had told Karsten, "You're in India now. Whatever is done will have to be done by the Indian government." But the ambassador, despite his pessimistic response, must have pulled the right strings, because the next morning a medical taxi took them to an airport, where they were provided with tickets to New Delhi.

The doctor had sewed up Karsten's chin, and that was the beginning of a new look for him. Louise told him he wouldn't be able to shave his chin until the wound healed, and she suggested it might be a good time for him to start growing a beard. From that day forward, Karsten sported a trademark aluminum-colored goatee, which led to his being mistaken for Colonel Sanders of Kentucky Fried Chicken fame. Someone once referred to that goatee as "the eighth wonder of Arizona." The goatee, which covered the scar from the accident, evolved over the years into what appeared to be a golf-ball on the point of his chin.

Karsten, chin deeply cut and bruised, gingerly helped Louise into and out of the taxi, onto the plane, off the plane, into another taxi, back to the hotel in New Delhi to pick up their luggage, and finally onto another plane. Louise had two black eyes—which eventually left her entire face black-and-blue for days—an arm with deep lacerations, and multiple other wounds that made her move carefully and painfully.

Karsten shot a photo of her during that time, and when they got it back from the developers later, at first neither of them recognized her. Looking through the pictures, Karsten commented, "I don't remember this person at all."

Louise studied the photo and finally identified her dress. "That's me!" she exclaimed.

It was not a picture they showed others.

ON THEIR WAY HOME

The plan was to fly to Calcutta, then Burma, and finally on to the States, but given Louise's condition, they decided they didn't want to endure that much flying in a short time. Instead, they flew to Bangkok, where they had friends. Once there, however, they found it difficult to get flights out of the country as quickly as they had hoped. Fortunately, with each passing day, Louise began to feel a little better. She still looked as if she had been beaten up, and she was moving slowly, but eventually she decided that besides her arm wound, the worst of her injuries were cuts and bruises. Karsten offered to take her home, but she decided to finish the trip as originally planned.

In each new city, they visited a hospital and had her arm and nose checked and her dressings changed. In Singapore, friends took her to their personal doctor, who referred her to a specialist. He made a spider web dressing of surgical tape that pulled the arm wound together and allowed it to heal without stitches or surgery. Today the scar is barely noticeable.

The trip was hard on Louise, but in the end she was glad she hadn't rushed home. Both she and Karsten had enjoyed themselves in spite of the accident, and she felt each such trip was another solid building block in their relationship. They came to know each other in deeper ways and relied upon each other more than ever. They were becoming better friends.

Karsten celebrated his sixtieth birthday five days after the accident, and one of his favorite memories was of the safari in Africa where, from the Treetop Hotel, they watched the animals moving about in the night.

To Louise, the trip sometimes seems a long time past, and at other times her memories are so vivid that it seems as recent as yesterday.

LIFE GOES ON

Two years after their mishap-marred trip, the Solheims moved to a home on the Moon Valley golf course, and Louise began playing golf for the first time. She felt that swinging a golf club would help strengthen her injured left arm. Their home was—and is—very nice but modest, considering the wealth they acquired through Karsten Manufacturing. Anyone who knew Karsten wouldn't be surprised at that. He was never motivated by a desire for an opulent lifestyle. One time, for example, Louise wanted to buy him an expensive Rolex. Though he appreciated the gesture, his comment was, "That's too much for a watch. I won't wear it."

The mid-1970s brought more great change and advancement for the company and the family. In 1975, Sandra married Alex Aiken. And Lou, who had taken a two-year sabbatical after his tenure at IBM, joined Karsten Manufacturing, making him the last of the three sons to enter the company.

Karsten's face was becoming one of the most recognized on golf courses around the world. Because of the phenomenal success of Ping clubs and the widely broadcast TV commercials featuring him, he drew crowds as big as those watching the great pro players. Often those players were in his gallery, hoping for a moment with him. At the Masters tournament, officials asked him to sign autographs somewhere not so close to the course. He was sought after by the biggest celebrities in golf and even the entertainment industry. Bob Hope, Bing Crosby, Dinah Shore, Milton Berle—everyone wanted to play golf and be photographed with "Mr. Ping."

Karsten Manufacturing continued its meteoric growth through the rest of the '70s and into the early '80s. When the company introduced the Ping Eye2 in 1982, however, its immediate sales success was soon tempered by the big problem it created for the golf world, particularly the USGA.

Karsten designed his irons the way he had his putters. He wanted to make the game easier for pros and amateurs alike. The company was racing toward new peaks in sales and satisfied customers, but it was also producing clubs that were so scientifically advanced that competitors and even the USGA wondered if they had gone too far. Was it still a fair game, and did it still test the best skills of all players, when the clubs were so sophisticated that they seemed to cause everyone's game to improve?

Karsten assumed that everyone would love the game more if the clubs helped all players improve. There was nothing unfair about a great club, especially if anyone who wanted one had access to it. But this controversy wouldn't go away, and it all had to do with tiny grooves in the club faces.

It should be noted that the USGA changed the requirement for grooves to be V-shaped in their 1984 Rule Book to allow them to be square or U-shaped. They did this because almost all golf-club manufacturers had gone to the lost wax process of investment casting, which made true V-grooves almost impossible to cast. Hence the change in the rule.

When Karsten read this in the rule book, he immediately took full advantage of it.

14

A SMALL BUT VITAL PROBLEM

Conflicts with the World of Golf

In one of the great ironies in the history of Karsten Manufacturing, it was, in fact, Karsten Solheim's pursuit of excellence that would cause the biggest headache for Karsten Manufacturing in the 1980s.

Karsten was always interested in making a good product great and a great product even better. He was interested in making the game of golf easier for those who played—from the elite pros down to the weekend hackers. He was so interested in changing and improving his products that he would tinker with the design while the first versions of the club were being manufactured.

No change was made just for the sake of change or just to have something new to feature with every marketing season. There was a purpose for each change Karsten made in one of his clubs. He was always gunning for perfection, and he never felt he hit it. The pursuit was the thing, and that made every product better every time it changed.

And that led to his experimenting with the shape of the grooves found in the face of club heads.

THE PURPOSE OF GROOVES

Nearly all golf irons and woods have grooves on the golf-club head. Grooves are parallel indentations of the face of the golf club. Grooves are placed on golf-club heads for the same reason that treads are put on tires—specifically, to channel moisture and perhaps debris in order to maximize the contact the club face makes with the golf ball. The source of the moisture that needs to be channeled can be either water on the grass or moisture contained in the grass, particularly moisture forced out of the grass when hitting from the rough. When the moisture is not channeled, the flight of the ball becomes less predictable. Karsten's goal with all golf clubs his company developed was to provide "consistent" performance.

Karsten Solheim once determined that the ball is in contact with the club for about one-twenty-five-hundredth of a second upon impact. Extrapolate that out to the weekend duffer's game of 100 strokes, and the club is actually in contact with the ball for a quarter of a second over eighteen holes!

Karsten's attention to detail caused him to study virtually everything about a club in an attempt to make it better. That meant that if he could find any way to make that brief contact with the ball truer, he could improve his club. It meant progress in his quest for perfection. He had already changed the face of golf-club manufacturing with heel-and-toe-weighted putters and perimeter-weighted, investment-cast irons. Was there something in the grooves that could be enhanced?

FOLLOWING THE RULES

Not surprisingly, there were rules about the grooves on a golf club. For forty years the United States Golf Association (USGA) had outlined three simple requirements for the grooves on clubs accepted in their tournaments:

- The grooves had to be V-shaped.
- They could not be more than .035-inch wide.
- Each groove had to be at least three times the width of the groove away from the next groove.

A problem came when the way that irons were manufactured was changed. By 1970, Karsten had quit using forged iron heads and converted to the investment-casting process to make the irons. Most golf manufacturers soon followed him. When the golf-club head is forged, the grooves are stamped into the head of the club in the shape of a V. However, when club heads are manufactured using the investment-casting process, it is very difficult to make a sharp V-shaped groove. The bottom of the V tends to smooth out, and this results in more of a U shape.

The USGA recognized that making golf clubs using the investment-cast method was good for golf. As a result, in 1984, the USGA revised the rule for V-shaped grooves to allow for a groove that was squarer, like a three-sided box. Ever the innovator, Karsten Solheim immediately saw promise in this new wording. While other manufacturers were merely relieved to know that their new investment-cast irons had, in essence, been summarily ruled conforming, Karsten began to experiment with the revised ruling.

NEW INNOVATIONS

Rather than just accepting that his investment-cast irons would have squarer grooves, Karsten designed purposely molded square grooves into his 1985 Ping Eye2 irons. He believed that more defined grooves would improve his clubs. The idea was that he wanted each dimple of a golf ball to, in some part, contact the club face directly over a groove.

U-grooves as manufactured by Karsten represented an improvement over V-grooves, because the width of the groove and the space between grooves stays the same as the head of the golf club wears down from play. As a result, even when Ping Eye2 irons with U-grooves begin to wear down, they more consistently play as they did when they were new, whereas V-groove irons do not perform like new as they wear out.

Karsten's improved clubs were gaining in popularity. However, the edges (or radii) of the first U-groove Ping Eye2 irons put small nicks into the golf ball. This caused a belief among golfers and golf professionals that the U-grooves were significantly increasing backspin on short chip shots.

The cut golf balls were a problem. Titleist executives contacted Ping reps to find a solution. Karsten solved that by slightly rounding off the edges of the grooves. Here, again, he was following the USGA rules, which stated that there can be no sharp edges on the face of the golf club.

The popularity of Ping Eye2 irons with U-grooves continued to increase dramatically. Golf-club manufacturers competing with Karsten began switching to U-grooves as well. However, this left many manufacturers with large inventories of unsold V-groove irons. Karsten had no unsold inventory of V-groove irons because he did not make a club until it was sold—then it was custom fit to the buyer's specifications. Many non-Ping players, including some professional PGA Tour players who had an economic stake in the sale of golf clubs by Karsten's competitors, began complaining that the Ping Eye2 irons were so good they gave less skilled players a competitive advantage over more skilled golfers.

Karsten felt that the argument was ridiculous on its face. He reasoned that if everyone played with similar equipment, the better golfer should win. Moreover, statistics from the PGA Tour showed that scores had not been significantly lowered as a result of the introduction of game-improving equipment. What Karsten had accomplished was the development of a golf club that would continue to play like new for far longer than the equipment historically made by his competitors.

But when the USGA studied the square grooves of the Ping Eye2s, it argued that Karsten's "rounding off" the sharp edges of the groove made the grooves wider so they would not cut the ball (we're talking the width of a human hair). Frank Thomas, the USGA technical director, also argued that rounding off the edges of the grooves made the grooves closer together. For that reason, he said that the grooves in the Eye2s violated the rule that they must be three times their width from one another.

Karsten and Louise didn't understand the USGA's argument. The USGA had always determined the width of a groove by measuring from the point where a horizontal line on the face of the club would intersect a vertical line extending along the wall of the groove. When using that "intersecting planes" method of measurement, Karsten's Ping Eye2 irons conformed to all rules regarding the maximum width of a groove and the minimum distance between grooves.

As the groove controversy grew, the USGA began conducting tests comparing U-groove irons and V-groove irons. Although the results of these tests showed some difference in spin rate between U-grooves and V-grooves, the USGA did not find that U-grooves conferred an unfair advantage. However, the USGA did conclude that placing grooves closer together would significantly increase spin rate. Thus the USGA adopted a new method for measuring groove widths (which correspondingly impacted the distance between grooves), called the "30-degree method of measurement."

The 30-degree method of measurement was not based on any engineering or scientific principles. Karsten believed it was adopted because the application of this unscientific measurement resulted in his Ping Eye2 irons being just barely on the "nonconforming" side of the line. The so-called "30-degree rule" also resulted in the USGA's abandoning its previous method of measuring groove widths, the "intersecting planes method"—the method specifically relied upon by Karsten in developing the Ping Eye2 irons with U-grooves.

The USGA wanted Karsten to narrow his grooves by the width of a human hair in order to conform to the USGA's new 30-degree rule. Karsten said no. The 30-degree rule made no sense. He said the grooves should be measured from the wall of the groove, rather than the edge. After all, any machinist knows that the way to measure the width of a beveled groove is to measure inside the groove, from wall to wall, and not from two points chosen entirely at random that are on the rounded edges.

The USGA threatened to outlaw the Ping Eye2s in tournament play. Karsten, who had already seen the club become the fastest-selling iron in history, was adamant. The Solheim stubbornness was tested and found still healthy and operative. He would not budge, and the USGA seemed to fear a lawsuit.

Finally, during the summer of 1987, the USGA made its ruling. The USGA announced that beginning in 1996, the 30-degree method of measurement would be mandatory, and all clubs not meeting it would be deemed nonconforming. In making this announcement, the USGA singled out the Ping Eye2 iron as the standard of nonconformity. Ironically, the USGA were unable to devise a tool to accurately measure conformity or nonconformity to their 30" rule.

The USGA also ruled that other golf associations, such as the PGA Tour, could impose this 30-degree rule (and thus ban Ping Eye2 irons) as early as January 1, 1990, and that the 30-degree rule would be used to determine which clubs could be used at the U.S. Open and other USGA events, beginning in 1990. Many experts believe the USGA refrained from immediately adopting a complete ban on Ping Eye2 irons in the hope that it would keep Karsten from filing a lawsuit.

WILL HE OR WON'T HE SUE?

Over the next two years, Karsten refused to give up hope that those in charge of the USGA would understand the correctness of his position. However, sometimes being right is not enough. The Ping Eye2 irons had become the most popular irons in the history of golf. This angered some of his competitors, many of whom had relationships with PGA Tour players who were very influential in the world of golf. Karsten was not a part of this inner circle. Those in charge of the USGA appeared determined not to back down to this relative newcomer, even if he was right. The USGA continued on its path of ruling that the golf clubs of millions of Karsten's customers would soon be nonconforming under the USGA Rules of Golf.

By the summer of 1989, the test of wills was reaching fever pitch. Karsten would not back down. His Ping Eye2 irons conformed to the Rules of Golf when made and were only being made nonconforming as a result of a highly questionable and unscientific rule. However, he feared that the professional golfers who played with his product, and thus interested amateurs in buying the same clubs, would soon abandon his Eye2 irons if they could not play with them in the thirteen USGA events such as the U.S. Open and the U.S. Senior Open. Karsten was also adamant about supporting the millions of golfers who had purchased his Eye2 irons. Following two years of impasse, Karsten brought suit against the USGA in August 1989.

In 1989, the PGA Tour decided to go the USGA one better. The PGA Tour voted to ban all square-grooved irons, beginning in 1990. As a result, Karsten sued the PGA Tour in late 1989, and in December of 1989 (just days before the PGA Tour's ban of U-grooved irons was to take effect), a federal court judge issued an injunction preventing the PGA Tour from banning these clubs until a full trial could be heard on the merits.

Ultimately, Karsten's persistence began to be rewarded. In late January 1990, he settled with the USGA. As part of that settlement, he obtained what he wanted most—to protect the millions of his customers who had purchased Ping Eye2 irons with U-grooves. Specifically, the USGA agreed that all Ping Eye2 irons with U-grooves made by Karsten would forever conform to the Rules of Golf (whether they conformed to the 30-degree rule or not). In return, Karsten agreed that within a few months of the settlement, he would narrow the width of his grooves by approximately the width of a human hair.

However, that settlement did not resolve the PGA Tour's continued efforts to ban all U-groove irons. Over the next three years, Karsten incurred huge legal fees in order to establish that the PGA Tour's intended ban of U-groove irons was improper. After he had won nearly every factual and legal battle in the case, on the eve of trial the PGA Tour relented and agreed that it would not ban U-groove irons. The PGA Tour was also required to pay Karsten money in an amount that remains confidential. Finally, in April 1993, the groove wars were over.

The war took a toll on Karsten, who was not a young man when it began. The controversy, which lasted nearly five years, had consumed him. He told a reporter that he thought about it "all day and much of the night." Many who were close to him at the time felt that it aged him quickly. It sapped him, at least temporarily, of the joy he derived from designing and manufacturing golf clubs.

Karsten hated the fact that the issue had gotten to the point of a lawsuit. He didn't want the lawsuit—as a businessman he saw lawsuits as a sometimes necessary evil—and he liked this legal wrangling even less. All he wanted to do, after all, was make the game of golf better.

Karsten did not want to bring out a new club design until he cleared the name of the Ping Eye2, and that kept him from introducing any new models during the groove controversy. In fact, the time he spent with the lawsuit made it impossible for him to do the things he loved to do with his company: spend time in the shop working with engineers on new designs. One has to wonder what more his fertile mind might have dreamed up if he had not been so distracted for so long.

Louise also felt that the legal battles were, at the very least, part of what caused Karsten to lose sight in his right eye. Two weeks after Deane Beman, the PGA Tour commissioner, announced the ban of all square-groove irons at PGA Tour events, Karsten, flying back from Seattle with Louise, thought he was seeing flashing lights. He asked Louise if she saw them, and she answered, "No."

Louise remembered her ophthalmologist's telling her that if she ever saw flashing lights to get to his office as soon as possible. Karsten was in the ophthalmologist's office at 7:30 the next morning, but it was too late. A tiny blood clot lodged on the optic nerve in his right eye, and there was nothing that could be done by that time. After that, he could only see shadows with the eye, and that was it.

15

THEY CALL
HIM "KARSTEN"

*Karsten Solheim
and His Workers*

Anyone who is familiar with the name Karsten Solheim is familiar with his innovations in golf-club designs. Everybody is familiar with heel-toe weighting and balance in his putters, investment casting and perimeter weighting with his irons, and the Ping Man, an ingenious contraption that simulates the motion of a human swing, making accurate testing of clubs easier.

But there was more to the way Karsten ran his business. Anyone who worked for or with Karsten Solheim, anyone who had a business relationship with him, knew that he was a man of uncompromising character and fairness. He treated all his associates very well, some say to a fault at times. His employees he treated with respect and dignity, and his business associates he treated with loyalty and fairness.

There was a reason for all that, and it stemmed from the most important thing in Karsten's life. It wasn't his golf-club business, and it wasn't even his wife or his children.

When Karsten Solheim started designing and building golf putters nearly half a century ago, his motivation was simple: He wanted to make golf easier for people. He wanted to make sure no golfer's equipment was a hindrance to his or her game. As a result, he had the pleasure of seeing professional golfers win hundreds of tournaments.

Underlying all that, though, were the principles that were pivotal in Karsten's life, and those principles can be found in the Bible. Karsten Solheim loved God and the Bible, and that was central in everything he did in his business—from how he carried on his financial affairs to how he dealt with every last one of his employees. Karsten was never a man who voiced his faith as much as he was one who showed it in his actions. He always tried to do right by everyone he knew. He wasn't perfect, but he had a love for people that motivated him always to treat them with respect and dignity.

A DIFFERENT KIND OF BOSS

Imagine a boss who is happy to give you a chance to earn a good living working for him, who treats you fairly in every way, who encourages you to enjoy your work and does all he can to ensure that you do, who gives you every opportunity for advancement, who treats you like a member of his own family, who forgives and encourages you when you make a mistake, and who knows and cares when you are sick or have family problems.

Does that seem a little backward from what corporate America has become? Well, like everything else he did, part of the unusual way Karsten Solheim ran his business was how he treated those who played the most vital role in his success: the employees.

Anyone who knew Karsten Solheim will tell you that he derived great joy from the success of his company simply because it allowed him to provide opportunities for people to earn a good living so that they could care for their families. That, say those who work at Karsten Manufacturing, was foremost in his mind.

"It's funny," says Bob Driescher, who began working for Karsten in January 1967, "but sometimes that seemed to be his number one priority—providing jobs for people." Driescher would know about those things. He's seen thousands of people hired in his thirty-plus years with the company.

One of the first employees when Karsten Manufacturing came into existence was Karsten's brother, Ray, who had been out of touch with the family for some years. In November 1966, Karsten received a phone call from his stepmother. "We've heard from Ray," she said. "He's in the Washington, D.C., area. He's broke and needs help. He's your brother, Karsten. You should help him." "I won't send him money," Karsten said. "But I'll send him a plane ticket and give him a job with us." Ray arrived with all his worldly goods in a brown paper grocery bag. Early in 1967, Ray went to work for Karsten.

As the company grew, Karsten was able to provide more and more well-paying jobs for people. But if there was one thing he didn't like about the incredible growth of his company, it was that it took away somewhat from what had been a "family" atmosphere at Karsten Manufacturing. Karsten had always been very family oriented, and he did all he could to make the atmosphere in the company like that of a family.

The company grew from fifteen employees—not counting the actual Solheim family—where Karsten knew everyone on a first-name basis, and a little something about each person's life, to about two thousand. It was impossible for him, or any other human for that matter, to maintain the personal feeling of the company after it had grown that large. And it bothered him.

From the very beginning, Karsten Manufacturing was a remarkably informal place to work. Karsten Solheim was never the kind of boss who looked at his employees as anything but family. Frankly, he didn't like that word *employees.* He was fond of telling them that there were no bosses in his company. To him, the people who worked for him were valuable just because they were people, just because they wanted to work to make things better for their families. And they should feel that they could come to him with problems.

He told his employees that they should put God number one in their lives, with their families second. The job, he said, should be behind that somewhere. He wanted people to enjoy their jobs. In fact, he would move workers around to match them with jobs they enjoyed or were proficient at. But he wanted them to understand that there was plenty in life they needed to put ahead of their work.

The words "human resource" would never leave Karsten's lips, and he never wanted "Mr. Solheim" to leave any of his employees' lips. He never wanted to be called anything but "Karsten." That, after all, was his name! Why wouldn't someone call him that? He wanted his employees to feel comfortable talking to him about anything from their personal and work-related problems to how things could run better for the company. He always lent an ear to suggestions. He very rarely followed up on them—remember, his personality was such that he wanted new ideas to be *his* ideas—but he listened.

Karsten was never a respecter of position. He believed that people were people, and it showed in how he promoted and in how he doled out company bonuses. His approach to filling positions was to hire from within, to promote talented people who had the ability, if not yet the know-how, to do a job given the opportunity. He rarely—some say never—hired from outside to fill positions when he had people he could promote.

Karsten's method of giving bonuses was revolutionary. He believed that every employee from the highest-ranking front-office personnel to the night janitor played an equally important part in the company's success and that, therefore, each should get the same amount when it came time for bonuses.

In the early '70s, when the company was growing at a rate of 25 percent a year, he wanted to share the wealth with the employees, and he asked someone to come in and set up a profit-sharing program. The man set up a traditional program, where the highest-paid employees got the biggest bonuses, based on percentages. "That's not what I want!" Karsten said. "I want everybody from the janitor on up to get the same. What we'll do is base it on how long they've been with us. After they've been with us two years, everybody gets the same number of points."

In addition, he also set up a pension/retirement program for his employees.

He was the owner of Karsten Manufacturing. Everyone who worked there, from the time there were fifteen employees early on to the time the payroll swelled to more than two thousand people, knew that Karsten Solheim was the boss. He may have been one of the most visible bosses in the history of American business. He was in the plant early every day, walking around, checking out how things were going, talking with people, giving instructions, and in general just being as visible and accessible as he could be. Karsten was a master at MBWA—Management By Walking Around. He once stopped a huge shipment to Japan because he noticed a grip put on not quite straight. The boxes were opened and the putter regripped. He personally showed the workers how to put on a grip.

A HANDS-ON, BENEVOLENT BOSS

Except when he was traveling, scarcely a day went by at Karsten Manufacturing when the boss wasn't there, walking around, talking to people, giving instructions, and taking input. He hired good people to do the work that needed to be done, but that didn't mean he wasn't going to be a part of what was going on every day in his company. He was a very hands-on, involved business owner, even as the company grew larger.

Karsten's employees knew they could be comfortable with him around. They knew that anything he wanted them to do, and any way he wanted them to do it, would probably be the right way. He was a demanding boss, but he was also fair. People knew what was expected of them, and what was expected was reasonable, even if it was at times nonnegotiable. He was strict in many ways. For example, he didn't allow cursing or swearing on the premises and later installed a "no smoking" policy—without being autocratic. He would listen to what an employee had to say, but he still wanted everything done his way.

Many people who knew Karsten will tell you that he was not great when it came to communicating verbally. He'd rather *show* you than *tell* you. He was like that when it came to relating to his employees. Rather than tell someone how to do something or have a supervisor do it, he was more likely to walk over, say hello to the employee, say, "Let me show you how to do this," then demonstrate how he wanted something done. Then he'd step back and let the employee do what he had just shown. "There! That's the way I like it," he'd say, then move on.

In the office, Karsten was obsessive about customer service. If there was one thing he couldn't stand, it was an unanswered phone. Company legend says that if you were on one line and unable to answer another that was ringing, Karsten himself would appear out of nowhere to take the call. He often glided through the customer service area and enjoyed getting on the phone. Customers couldn't believe it was really Karsten at first. Something that a company rep had just told them—and had made them frustrated—sounded better coming from the voice from the top. A rep saying your order would take several more weeks was nothing like the boss man himself apologizing for the delay due to the popularity of the club you ordered.

Even when an employee made a mistake—and there was no way to completely eliminate mistakes in a company of that size—Karsten would correct the person but in a way that kept the worker's dignity intact. For example, once when the company was just starting, someone dropped a vise on the floor of the new building, gouging a hole in the brand-new tile. Karsten didn't tear into the employee, and he didn't appear to be angry. He simply looked at him and said, "What are you doing?" "I dropped the vise, and it fell on the floor," the employee said. Karsten continued looking at the employee and said, "Did you expect it to fall *up?*" Karsten was upset at the mistake, but he made light of it, at the same time giving the person the message to be more careful.

Karsten absolutely detested firing people. He cared too much about people to terminate them without giving them every opportunity to rehabilitate themselves. He was the boss of second, third, fourth, and fifth chances. Firing someone in a company like Karsten's was something like turning out a member of the family, and he hated doing it. To him, there weren't a lot of workplace problems that couldn't be worked out, even if it meant moving an employee to another area of the company.

Like any employer, Karsten Manufacturing would occasionally hire "bad seeds," people who didn't want to work hard or whose moral and ethical bearings weren't right. They perhaps were habitually absent from work, or, when they did show up, they didn't work hard. But Karsten wouldn't fire them without giving them every opportunity to straighten up. He saw in every person the potential to be a good employee. He believed that in every person's heart there was the desire to do what was right. Sometimes he was right about that; other times he had to bite the bullet and let someone go, though he always did it with a sad heart.

Even employees who had personal conflicts with Karsten were given every chance to stay with the company. One machinist he had hired would have daily arguments with him that sometimes led to shouting matches. Even though the two men disagreed about nearly everything, there was a mutual respect between them. At another company, the man would have been fired, but Karsten wouldn't do that. Things improved dramatically when he added a new machinist, named Wil Harwood, to the company. Wil was able to take Karsten's ideas and create the molds the way Karsten wanted them.

In the early '70s, an emotionally unbalanced employee created problems. She was a paranoid schizophrenic who twice attacked her foreman and once chased John's future wife around the shop with a golf club. Karsten felt compassion for this sick woman and did all he could to figure out a way to keep her on the payroll. He wouldn't give up on her. Finally, after many episodes, with a sad heart he had to let her go.

One thing he absolutely would not tolerate was theft from the company by an employee. Bob Driescher remembers that as being rare, since Karsten treated his employees so well that few ever felt the need to steal. Even then, Karsten would talk to the offender and try to offer his forgiveness, if the employee said the right things to him.

Although the way he handled his employees may seem

unorthodox, to say the least, the results in the workplace were remarkable. He was respected among those who worked for Karsten Manufacturing, but he was also looked at affectionately. The employees loved the man, even seeing him as something of a father figure. They felt a part of his family. For that reason, Karsten Manufacturing kept many long-term, loyal employees, and they stayed that way because they felt wanted, needed, and rewarded.

None of this meant Karsten was easy to work with. Bob Cantin, his longtime director of communications and advertising, reaffirms that Karsten's strengths could be his weaknesses. He was so obsessed with improving things that he would see something he wanted changed in an ad that had already appeared in a magazine and would insist that it be adjusted before it appeared again.

At Karsten Manufacturing, Cantin says, change was constant because Karsten was always trying to upgrade the product. He was a perfectionist who demanded excellence. Yet Cantin also sees Karsten Solheim as having been "one of the most humble men I have ever met."

His other employees would probably agree.

A poignant letter, written in 1986, concerning the early days of the company came from one of the first employees. He remembered an incident that typified the way Karsten was with his employees, his family:

> We were still in the original building and we had a foreign order for putters that had to be shipped that day. Some of the putters were late coming in from the foundry, so when they arrived, we all got busy.
>
> The crew at that time consisted of Rick Hepler, Bill Miller, Frank Kakrada, Gilberto Peralta, John Keeney, Jack Otten, Nel Tooker, and Diane and Karen (whose last names I don't remember). Of course John Solheim was there, and naturally Karsten, who was right in there with us.

After the putters were ground and put in the tumbler for two hours, Karsten and Louise took us all out to dinner at the restaurant on the corner of 19th Avenue and Peoria. After dinner we all went back and worked late into the evening. At about ten o'clock the order was finished and John and Rick and I took it to the airport.

It's still the same today as it was then, everybody working together as a team. The people do this because Karsten and Louise make them feel like part of the family. No matter how successful they become, they still base everything on honesty and integrity with their customers and their employees. Many of us owe a great deal to them and to their families.

I know this sounds a little pretentious, but we don't very often get a chance to express how we feel about them.

Bob Driescher

FIGHTING LAYOFFS

Layoffs weren't a fact of life for Karsten Manufacturing early on, because the company was expanding rapidly and hiring. But later they became necessary. When orders slowed, Karsten would do all he could before laying anyone off, putting production employees on make-work jobs—pulling weeds or painting or sweeping the parking lot—to keep from having to let them go.

Although Karsten and his sons, who were moving into higher positions of managership during the '70s and '80s, did all they could to avoid layoffs, there came a time in the mid '90s when layoffs were a sad fact. When the company first started selling the Eye2 irons, the payroll expanded. As the business moved into golf-ball production and other areas, there was a high of more than two thousand working for Karsten Manufacturing. But eventually, as much as Karsten hated it, as much as it broke his heart, a layoff had to happen.

Other golf-club manufacturers had begun emulating

Karsten's products, cutting into his sales. The company got to a point where it had to cut back to the basics: woods, irons, putters, and golf bags. The family and those still working at Karsten Manufacturing—roughly fifteen hundred work there now—remember isolating him from the layoffs. They all knew Karsten, and they knew that if he had to handle the layoffs, he would be devastated. They knew he couldn't bear to see people leave the complex for a final time, knowing they would be on their own to look for work.

It was a rough time for Karsten, Louise, and their sons. Still, the layoffs took place. The company gave each person it had to let go an excellent severance package, counseling, and job placement assistance. Life went on, both for those who had to leave and for the company.

In fact, as the company moved into the '90s, Karsten was on the verge of facing the biggest challenge of his life.

LIFE AT THE TOP

Ping was at the top of the golf-club manufacturing world throughout the '80s, and the club was represented in a special closet at the plant. Karsten had a storage area—actually, it was more of a vault—in which he placed a gold-plated Ping putter for every professional tour tournament victory worldwide. After a golfer won a pro event with a Ping putter, Karsten would gold plate two putters and inscribe the name of the event, the winner's name, and the date of the victory. He would then give one putter to the golfer and put the other in his closet. To date there are more than eighteen hundred putters in that closet.

Ping was indeed at the top, but the competition was becoming fierce. It didn't seem so many years before that Karsten was producing the only heel-and-toe-weighted putters and perimeter-weighted irons in the industry. Now companies either crafted their clubs that way, or they were soon out of business.

Karsten kept looking for newer and better ways to improve his clubs. With son Lou running the computer area and Karsten Engineering, Allan handling personnel and running several subsidiary companies, and John in marketing production and research and development, Karsten and Louise had seen their family business come to fruition. Daughter Sandra worked. His brother, Ray, worked part-time. And observers could sense the "family feel" even among the nearly two thousand other employees who were not related.

Karsten had grown and matured with age, though there was no pretending he hadn't missed out on a lot of good opportunities as a parent. His reputation as an elder statesman of golf and an innovative genius went well with his kindly and generous nature.

There were, however, forces outside Karsten Manufacturing that threatened its perch at the top of the industry. Experts within and without the company realized that these needed to be dealt with, but how did one initiate change in an organization run so long by one man his way?

By the mid-1990s, while Karsten Manufacturing was still one of the leaders and *Forbes* still ranked Karsten among the 400 wealthiest people in the United States, the business landscape had changed. For more than twelve years, Ping had sold the best-selling iron on the market. Now its iron was number two. Orders had fallen enough to force more than one hundred to be laid off in Phoenix for the second time in the company's history.

Some criticized Ping advertising as being old-fashioned and pedestrian. Their ads featured Karsten and trumpeted his innovative genius and the quality of Ping products. That was good, but it was not as sophisticated as the newer competition's. Competitors were making claims that their clubs were better and, without saying so, that Ping was behind the times.

The sad fact was that, though the competitors' ads exaggerated the quality of their clubs, the claim that Ping was behind the times was true. Everyone seemed to know this except Karsten. And now, it wasn't because he was being belligerent or stubborn or simply wanted to do everything his own way. There was another complicator, and at first it was known only to Louise.

16

CHANGES AT THE TOP

Dealing with a Life-Changing Illness

As surprising as it may be to those who didn't know him, Karsten Solheim never had a great memory. In fact, he complained all his life of having a bad memory. It became legendary and even a joke at times.

Karsten was a dreamer, a visionary. He could look at something and see an end result—sometimes instantly. The details required to get from point A to point B were sometimes beyond him, only because he might forget them. Names were a problem, as were dates and other incidental bits of information useless to his overall dreams of perfecting golf clubs. Those who are familiar with Karsten Manufacturing will tell you that is where Louise played a large role in the administration of the company. It was she who handled the details, the ones Karsten would surely have forgotten on his own.

But as the mid-'90s rolled around, something about Karsten became different. His memory got much worse. He began forgetting things he had never forgotten before. His short-term memory became even shorter. At home, sometimes from one moment to the next he would forget what he had been talking about, become unable to find the right word, ask several times about their plans for a meal or for an evening out. Gradually losing his ability to focus and remember and make correct word choices frustrated him. He might become cross. But again, this seemed to have nothing to do with his old ways of doing things.

A SERIOUS CONDITION

At first Louise tried to pass off Karsten's increasingly bad memory as the result of age. After all, he was well into his eighties now, and it wasn't at all uncommon for people to lose their ability to remember at that age. But she realized quickly that this was more than just some limited case of premature senility. Although it wasn't severe at first, she admitted to herself that a degree of dementia had crept into her husband's brilliant mind.

Louise, it turns out, was right. Karsten wasn't just getting old; he was a very sick man. The Rochester Mayo Clinic diagnosed him as having Parkinson's disease with dementia.

As time went on, his condition grew steadily worse. He who had signed so many autographs was now unable to write or even sign his own name. Cards were made with his picture and facsimile signature and a brief bio, which he handed out. One day he was unable to differentiate between the telephone and the doorbell. His train of thought often wandered, and sometimes he merely stopped speaking in midsentence when he forgot what he was talking about. He would get up in the middle of the night and walk around the house. A few times, he had his suitcases out, ready to pack for a trip only he knew about. Louise didn't sleep much during that time.

Karsten still had his routines. He wanted to go to work. He wanted to be in on meetings. He wanted to manage by walking around. But the man who used to be able to pick an unmarked key from a huge ring of keys and open an unmarked door now sometimes walked through doors and seemed lost in his own complex.

The deterioration of Karsten's mind was gradual, but it got to the point where he became much less communicative and needed more constant attention. How ironic that a man who had been characterized by genius and who had made his fortune largely with his mind now saw it betray him in his twilight years.

Louise had seen him make major strides and changes in his relationship toward her, and she was grateful for that. Even during the toughest times of their marriage, when "kid troubles" and differences in time priorities, and especially Sandra's trauma, caused tremendous tension in the marriage, she had never lost her love for him. Though there had been a time when she wondered if she could go on, the thought of separation or divorce was unthinkable to her. She had made a commitment, she believed in him, and she knew that while they may have disagreed on some points, he would come around and do what was right.

For years Karsten had been Louise's rock. He was the one who knew how to do things. He was the one who could make decisions. She had centered her life on helping him and supporting him. Now, gradually and yet all too suddenly for her, she realized he was becoming dependent upon her.

Before this, she had enjoyed some independence. They had spent much time together and had traveled together, but she could run out to her own appointments, have lunch with friends, attend meetings, or whatever she liked whenever she wanted to. Now Karsten seemed extremely eager to always know where she was. It was as if he needed her to simply manage his life.

A DIFFERENT MAN

Realizing that Karsten Solheim was not the man he once was came as an alarming truth to his many friends, employees, colleagues, and even acquaintances. He had been known widely as a gregarious, people-oriented, fun-loving person. Now, when he and Louise went to a restaurant, he might revert to his old ways. He would stride straight to the maitre d' or waiter and greet him, find his favorite table, and order his usual. But when that person tried to engage him in conversation, Louise was never quite sure what Karsten understood and what he didn't. Sometimes the old alertness returned, and he would engage in repartee. But at other times he might start one story and finish another. Sometimes he mumbled, or his conversation trailed off. It pained her to see on the faces of those who were talking to him the realization that something was wrong.

A CHANGE AT THE TOP

It became obvious to everyone that the time had come to turn over the reins of the company to one of the sons. Lou was the eldest but had not expressed interest in running the company. Allan was next in line agewise but saw his own gifts more in the supporting and guiding areas. John, though youngest, was no rookie. He had been with the company since its inception and had been fashioning clubs and helping his father design them for years.

In 1995, the day came when change was inevitable. John was going to take over the company. There was no way it wasn't going to happen, but it would certainly be neither clandestine nor hostile. John had the permission and the blessing of his father to take over. The details of that conversation will never be known, because John considered it between himself and his father. However, whatever went on behind closed doors made for a smooth, though long overdue, change of power.

Near the end of a company board meeting, John simply stated, "I would like to nominate Karsten as chairman of the company, and I would like Karsten to nominate me as president." Karsten immediately agreed and said so, Allan seconded the nominations, and the vote was unanimous. The change had been coming for a decade, and now it was suddenly done.

Lou was named president of Karsten Engineering. Allan became executive vice president of Karsten Manufacturing, reporting directly to his younger brother, John. And life went on.

CHANGES IN THE COMPANY

On the business side, John immediately changed several things for the better. He was in no way disparaging his father's legacy to the company, but he was acknowledging that they had fallen behind in advertising and promotion and even in technology. He feared they had lost ground during the lawsuit over the grooves controversy, and it was time to come out with a new design to recapture some of the lost iron market.

John hired an advertising agency and began promoting the new Ping iron, the ISI. The first ad read, "For thirty-seven years, the Solheim family has gone to work and said, 'How can we make a better golf club?' Recently, they had a particularly good day at the office." The ad also carried a picture of John with his father and added that the ISI was John's own design, his first iron. The copy says, "It's the next generation from the next generation."

The rest of the golf world had waited anxiously for something new from Ping. Most conceded that any blip in the graph of Karsten Manufacturing's success was just a glitch and that the company would come roaring back into competition. The years would have to determine that, as they relentlessly took a toll on the mind of the founder and chairman.

CARING FOR KARSTEN

Louise, who had been trying for years to spend less time in the office, now was really able to. She still served in many important capacities but felt that her major responsibility was giving care to Karsten.

There were days when he was unaware that anything was wrong. He would get up and want to go to work, and Louise would call someone to drive them to the plant. Karsten might wander. He might visit the factory. He might chat with employees or customers. He liked to visit the engineering department.

Sometimes he would ask a visitor whom he wanted to see, would mistake the name for someone who had worked at the company years before, and be in danger of directing him to the wrong area. There was always someone to watch for just that, and no damage was done.

Still friendly and fascinated by people, Karsten would often be more interested in the conversation at the table next to him in a restaurant than he was in the conversation at his own. Louise found herself having to sneak off to appointments while he was otherwise engaged so as not to upset him with her absence. In a strange way, she was grateful for the opportunity to finally serve him. She had long ago vowed to love him for better or for worse, for richer or for poorer, in sickness and in health. She had not had to fulfill that vow until now. She was determined to do it, not grudgingly but with a smile. To care for Karsten was for her a joy, and he knew it.

The day would come when Karsten would not be able

to go where he wanted to go, and he certainly would not be able to play much golf or travel internationally. But until that time, Louise determined that she would try to keep his life as full and as active and engaged as possible.

As of late 1998, Karsten would still tell her that he wanted to travel, to Norway, for example, to visit family. But for the first time since they had started the business, such trips were no longer practical. He just required too much care, care Louise was not able to give on her own.

She continued to disengage from the company to let her sons take care of it. Advancing age has cost Louise much of her eyesight, which once allowed her to read as much as she wanted and write long, handwritten letters to her friends and loved ones. While she may have lost a step or two and is not as mobile as she once was, her mind and spirit seem not to have suffered. She remains bright and sharp with an excellent memory and delightful wit. People around her love her, her ability to articulate, and her sparkling smile.

There was one thing that Karsten Solheim had not forgotten. Whenever he heard the song "You Are My Sunshine," he beamed from ear to ear, took Louise's hand, and sometimes even sang along. When everything else in that well-worn mind seemed to have tumbled from the filing cabinets and become more and more difficult to assimilate, something told him that was their song.

Louise still adored the man with whom she had spent more than six decades of her life, but she was realistic about his chances for improvement. She realized that Karsten's condition would probably never improve, at least in the long run. He had days when he was more alert than others, but he also had down days. He required constant attention, which was provided twenty-four hours a day by health care professionals.

Early in 1998, Karsten had a close brush with death

when a serious bout of pneumonia hospitalized him. He had a rough few months, and his family, those at Karsten Manufacturing and the ones who had been his friends over the years, breathed a sigh of relief that he survived.

This demonstrated what those closest to Karsten already knew: He was, with his imperfections and his humanity, a man who was deeply loved by those around him.

And he was a man who was leaving behind a legacy—for his family, his friends, his company, and the game of golf.

THE SOLHEIM LEGACY

Following in Karsten's Footsteps

Karsten Solheim was like any man who has undertaken anything worthwhile in his life: He wanted to be remembered for something. He wanted to know that he made a difference in whatever arena he worked in. He wanted to know that he was leaving behind something positive for his children and grandchildren.

In short, Karsten Solheim wanted to leave a legacy.

He certainly has done that.

By now you know that Karsten Solheim revolutionized the golf equipment industry. His club designs, his manufacturing techniques, and his use of simple physics changed forever the face of golf-club design. Now, at the beginning of the twenty-first century, the entire golf-club industry is doing the things he started. Virtually every successful putter on tour today has components of what you see in Karsten's drawing. Many are exact duplicates of that design. When the patent ran out, there was nothing anybody could do to keep people from copying it.

But there was more to this man than just the golf clubs. Anyone who knew Karsten knows that the golf clubs were what he made, not who he was. They know he was a man of uncompromising integrity and that he was a man who loved God and people. They know that in all he did, Karsten Solheim put God first, followed by people. They also know that he was a man who loved his wife, children, and the rest of his family, as well as other people around him.

That, in short, is Karsten's legacy. That is where he left his mark.

MAKING HIS MARK ON GOLF

By 1990 Karsten Solheim had long been the most famous golf-club manufacturer in the world. The entire industry had emulated him. He was revered, feared, and respected—albeit sometimes grudgingly—by the competition.

Times have changed in the golf-club industry. Karsten Manufacturing is making better clubs than ever, but the Pings are no longer alone at the top of the heap. Simply put, the competition has caught up—maybe caught *on*. Karsten's ideas—heel-toe weighting in the putters and perimeter weighting and investment casting for the irons, just to name two—were once radical. When his patents ran out on that technology, it was "open season," and nearly everyone copied what he had been doing for years. Indeed, many people look back at Karsten's way of doing business and say he should have been more protective of his patents. But now those things are the rule rather than the exception in golf clubs. Every major golf manufacturer—Armour, Wilson, Cobra, Callaway, Titleist, Spalding, Hogan, Taylor

Made—uses technology that at the very least got its start with Karsten.

There was more, though. Not only was Karsten Solheim a revolutionary when it came to how golf clubs were made; he was also an ambassador for the game, especially where it was most needed: women's golf.

GIVING THEM A FAIR BREAK

Karsten and Louise spent time every year traveling the country and the globe. They served as goodwill ambassadors for the United States, for golf, for their own company, for God as they visited missionaries everywhere, and in a large measure became avid fans and supporters of women's golf.

When asked why he spent so much of his time and energy promoting women's golf, Karsten simply said that the women needed the help. To him, it didn't seem the women's game got the attention it deserved. And, Karsten being Karsten, he wanted to provide the best women golfers in the world a showcase for their talents.

Bill Blue, commissioner of the LPGA at the time and a man the Solheims credit with getting a tournament started, asked Karsten and Louise if they would consider sponsoring a Ryder Cup kind of event for the women. After much thought and planning and preparation, Karsten and Louise announced their plan to underwrite a Ryder Cup style biennial tournament event that would pit the United States and European professional women's teams against each other.

As in other international team golf events, players from the United States and from Europe were selected through a point system based on tournament performance on the Ladies Professional Golf Association (LPGA) and the Women's Professional Golfers European Tour (WPGET), now the Ladies European Tour (LET). The first venue was eight players each, the second was ten, and since then it has been twelve, like the Ryder Cup.

Karsten Manufacturing agreed to underwrite the event ten times over the next twenty years, and, in tribute to Karsten, the teams would compete for what would be called The Solheim Cup. The cup itself was crafted in Ireland of Waterford crystal.

Commercials on television and advertisements in magazines announced the new tournament and added images of Karsten to the previous promotion for Ping clubs. He suddenly became almost as well known to the general public as he had to those inside the golf industry.

A GREAT START

A certain irony surrounded the beginning of The Solheim Cup competition. The first contest for the Cup was held in November 1990 at Lake Nona Golf Club in Orlando, Florida. Most experts, even in Europe, believed not only that the Europeans had no hope of beating the United States in this initial tourney, but they also wondered if Europe would be able to catch the Americans at all during those first twenty years.

British professional golf star Laura Davies believed and said otherwise, though most considered her pronouncement brash posturing. Before the opening ceremonies she said, "I'm prepared to wager anyone we will win."

Davies partnered with Alison Nicholas and won the first match of the first day against Americans Nancy Lopez and Pat Bradley. But that merely served to awaken the American Solheim Cup team, which went on to win the tournament easily. After losing to Betsy King and Beth Daniel in a second-day match, Nicholas complained, "It was like playing God and God."

Pat Bradley said, "There might come a point when the Europeans will be competitive in this format, but it won't be for a while."

The Solheim Cup, however, alternated between continents every two years, so in 1992 it was played at the Dalmahoy Hotel Golf and Country Club near Edinburgh, Scotland. Shockingly, in this, only the second contest for the Cup, Catrin Nilsmark of Sweden had a chance to clinch not only her match with American Meg Mallon but also to clinch a European triumph if she could sink a two-foot putt on the sixteenth green. When she made it, Europe had evened the score in Solheim Cup competition.

Mickey Walker, the European captain, said, "Whatever the Americans say, I think they believed they were going to come over here and win comfortably. I think they're probably in shock."

Such competition got the Solheim Cup off to a great start, and it quickly became one of the most anticipated and competitive professional golf tournaments in the world. Even today, the Solheim Cup provides an arena where the best women professional golfers represent their countries in the true competitive spirit of the game, which was precisely what Karsten Solheim had desired.

A GENEROUS GESTURE

Sponsoring such a contest with a heavy outlay of resources was a generous gesture, of course, but it also made great marketing and promotional sense for Karsten Manufacturing. Getting the Karsten Solheim and Ping names before an international audience through such a tournament and its attendant advertising only enhanced the company's reputation and increased sales.

However, for years Karsten and Louise had also been quietly making generous use of their resources for other causes around the world, causes that were clearly humanitarian, faith related, and not in any way designed to benefit them from a business standpoint.

The Solheims agreed to be a major donor to the Moody Bible Institute of Chicago to help finance a state-of-the-art physical education facility on MBI's inner-city campus. The Institute had been limping along for years with cramped and substandard physical education quarters.

Marrying the Solheims and their interest in sports with the need at Moody resulted in an ingenious match that produced one of the finest athletic complexes in the city. The Solheims had agreed to the project only on the condition that Moody propose a facility first-class in every detail. Once Karsten saw the plans for the beautiful basketball court, practice gyms, workout rooms, weight-training center, racquetball courts, and Olympic-sized swimming pool, he and Louise agreed to underwrite the cost. Moody Bible Institute honored this commitment by naming the facility the Solheim Center. The result is such a gem that the building is considered on a par with some of the finest in the world.

Several National Basketball Association teams work out at the Solheim Center when they come to town to play the Bulls. The NBA rookie camp has been held there more than once. Even the Dream Team, the U.S. Olympic basketball team made up of the best of the NBA, has practiced there. But, more important to the Solheims, the Institute has not kept the center exclusively for the use of its own students and NBA teams. MBI opens the building on selected days for the use of local, inner-city ministries, giving underprivileged children access to facilities they might not otherwise ever see, let alone play in. These ministries are, of course, evangelistic. The Solheims were thrilled to have a part in providing a place where such youngsters can come and also be exposed to the truths of God.

Several other Christian colleges have since also become recipients of gifts that have allowed them to construct similar Solheim Centers.

No one knows what kinds of donations Karsten and his wife gave to make various ministries possible. Karsten, even in his later years, wasn't one to talk about those things. To him, what a man gives and to whom is between him and God. He believed that his reward for the things he did on earth would be forthcoming in the next life.

THE FAMILY LEGACY

More visible to those who are familiar with Karsten's life, though, is what he left as a legacy for Karsten Manufacturing, his creation and his business. He left a legacy for the business but especially for those who have taken over running it: his sons.

Those who know Lou, Allan, and John Solheim respect and admire them in much the same way they respected and admired their father. Karsten and Louise instilled in their sons the kinds of values and principles that made their business and their lives a success. These bedrock principles that took Karsten from shoe repairman to engineer to dramatically successful entrepreneur and allowed him to live the American dream remain valuable for any student of life and business:

- Put God first in your life.
- A man's responsibility is to provide for his family.
- If you are the right kind of a person, there's no reason you shouldn't be happy. Happiness depends on you. Karsten had a button saying that made and passed out to the employees.
- Know who you are, what you want, and where you're going—and communicate it.
- Manage by walking around.
- If workers know the boss personally and are free to call him by his first name, they will be happier, healthier employees.

- While salaries necessarily vary, pay bonuses to everyone equally. They all work hard and are equally important to the company.

- Never abide shortcuts, shoddy work, or bargain buying at the expense of the final product.

- Never discount. Never mass market. Rather, manufacture product at the highest level possible and trust the discriminating buyer to rise to the appropriate price.

- People will pay for quality products made with quality materials by skilled workmen.

- The customer who likes your product and sees its benefits will be willing to pay for it.

- Aim toward customers who buy on the basis of quality, not price.

- There are plenty of so-called bargains out there.

- The only real bargain is quality at a fair price.

- Worry more about your own plans and dreams than about what the competition is up to. If you have a quality product, there will be room in the marketplace for it.

- Keep very limited inventories of finished product. Manufacture only custom-ordered merchandise.

- Always do your best on every piece you work on.

- Don't let one piece on which you could have done a better job go to the customer.

- Never ignore a ringing phone.

- Always stay busy. There's always something to do. Never sit around.

- There is not an engineering or design problem that cannot be solved, and there is not a discipline or sport that cannot be mastered.

These seem to be really basic principles. But they are principles that Karsten not only talked about but lived in both his personal and professional life. They are, after all, the things that made him what he became during the second half of his life.

They were Karsten's way.

AFTERWORD

The challenge was there. What would happen next depended on me. I had just been elected president of Karsten Manufacturing Corporation. The year was 1995, and I was forty-nine years old. Would I be able to fill the big shoes my father, Karsten Solheim, who was reluctantly leaving, and lead this amazing corporation into the next century? My dad had spent the last half of his life trying to make the game of golf easier for those who played it. He wanted nothing more than for people to enjoy playing the game he had learned to love. Everything he had done prior to developing that very first putter had laid the groundwork for what had become one of the most innovative golf manufacturing companies in the world.

I was thirteen years old and in the eighth grade when Dad designed that first putter, patented it, and began producing them in our garage. I was the youngest of four children, six years younger than my nearest sibling, Allan, who was about to graduate from high school and join the U.S. Marine Reserves. My sister, Sandra, was working at *Sunset* magazine. My oldest brother, Karsten Louis, was about to finish college with a degree in electrical engineering from the University of Wyoming, after which he would go to a position with IBM for many years. We all helped Dad with his new hobby whenever possible (if we were home to help) in those early days. But because I had a lot of school left, I was available to help almost always.

Even at that young age, I was intrigued by Dad's ingenuity and theories on how to make a golf putter roll the ball. He had the seemingly innate ability to do things he had never done before such as using the milling machine to do his own tool and die work, making molds to cast the putters, designing and making new machines to do work required. It was fascinating working with him, and being of a similar nature, mechanically inclined so to speak, I decided early on I had found my career and never considered working elsewhere.

Now I faced my challenge! Would I be able to carry on where Dad left off? I had hoped to work alongside him for a few more years, but the years had taken a toll on Dad. He was nearly eighty-four years old. Parkinson's Disease with dementia had slowly removed his sharpness; he did not want to make much needed changes. In the '70s and '80s, the company had started to diversify. We added an investment casting foundry, a heat treating plant, invested heavily into producing a top grade golf ball, a precision machining business, a turf research and service program, a country club, and even an out-of-state strip mall near Karsten and Louise's summer home in Washington state. Karsten also had started a separate facility in England to assemble and distribute Ping clubs there and in Europe, called Karsten UK.

One by one the whole family had become involved in the business, Sandra in 1966, Allan in 1967 and Louis in 1975. Now six or eight grandchildren or their spouses had joined our workforce, which numbered nearly 2,000. The lives of a lot of people would be affected by decisions made by the top at KMC. I felt the burden Dad and Mother had been carrying for many years. We were now feeling the pinch these heavy dollar investments made in businesses outside of our golf club core, but even more so they required a great deal of time from Karsten, my brothers Louis and Allan, and me. Worse, they were often a big source of conflict in the family. We didn't need that. Decisions had to be made.

The groove issue was another thing that had taken a heavy toll on Karsten. It had started in the middle '80s, and in 1990 Allan, Roy Freeman (Roy was Managing Director of Karsten UK), and I convinced Karsten to settle with the USGA, but it put a strain on Dad's relationship with me. It finally settled with the PGA Tour in 1993 out of court. Dad was a happy man when he reached out his hand to Deane Beman and said, "Can we say it's finished?" And Deane took his hand and replied, "Yes, Karsten, we can say it's finished."

Karsten was then almost eighty-two years old; he had not wanted to bring out a new model of irons until the name of the all-time best selling Eye2's had been cleared, but fortunately there was one last great set of irons that he designed and I helped with. This was the Zing 2 iron, which I feel overall was the most forgiving iron Ping has ever built. Kirk Triplett won with them on the PGA Tour the week Dad passed away. Lee Westwood also won with them on the European Tour this year and has had many other wins with them all over the world.

Dad let me know I wasn't keeping him up on things. I felt I was working hard to keep him informed, but nothing seemed to help. (Today this experience has helped me a lot when working with my own sons.) Many of us sensed that Karsten felt I was trying to take over, as he would quickly reject most of my ideas in design and business. After realizing this and accepting it, I learned to use others to present my ideas to him. It worked. I did get Dad to agree to make some changes to our previous iron. Fortunately for us, the computer age for design came along and with it a brilliant young engineer by the name of Dan Kubica. Dan did a great job of helping my dad and me work better together by very effectively explaining things to Karsten in a way that eliminated conflict. Karsten made all the final calls on the Zing 2 design, taking most of my ideas and adding many more of his own to build this great iron.

With the advent of extreme marketing in the golf industry, plus time spent on the groove issue and our non-core businesses, our engineering-based company had lost touch with the market. I didn't realize this until Doug

Hawken and I took a trip back to Boston for an LPGA tournament that we were co-sponsoring with Welch's. (At the time, Doug was director of marketing at KMC and later moved into the position of general manager. He first joined our firm in 1971 just out of college. He is now President of Ping.) We had roundtables with a number of our more active accounts and one of our best sales representatives, Peter Harrity. These roundtables helped us get a much better understanding of what was happening in the marketplace, and from this Doug and I set about to figure out how we could merge Karsten's ideals with modern marketing.

For the first time ever we hired a marketing agency, The Martin Group of Richmond, Virginia to help us. My father had revolutionized the golf industry in design, quality, and custom fitting. We had maintained our position as the leader in quality in our industry, but the marketing of our competition had succeeded in creating the perception that they had the superior design. We needed to regain our lead position.

My son John Karsten and Ping's engineering team have revitalized our lagging putter business with our new Isopur and IsoForce putters. Where they have succeeded in that marketplace is with the number of putters sold worldwide. However, since we do not pay players to use our putters, we are not where we would like to be with the number of putters on the U.S. tour. It has been frustrating to see our competition make exact copies of my father's designs, relabel them with someone else's name and pay players upwards of $1,000 per week to use Karsten's designs. I have set a goal that Ping will take my father's putter ideals to an even greater height and retake this as well.

We also realized we needed a lead product; where irons had been the lead product in the '80s, drivers were the lead product in the '90s. So we set to work building a great metal driver. It had to have all of Karsten's design features, be more forgiving, more fittable than anything else out there and as long in distance as any of the competition. When our team finished the Ping TiSI, we'd more than succeeded in our goal. The distance surprised even us. We knew we would be long, but twelve yards longer than the most popular club and six yards longer than anything else was beyond our dreams. It has been very gratifying that at the men's NCAA Championship this year, more than half of the players used our driver. Two years ago we had two.

This year we added a new set of irons that has many of the characteristics of Karsten's Eye2 iron, still the most popular iron of all time. The new iron, the i3, has more traditional optics than the Eye2 and more extreme weighting. But it needed to have a lead as well. For years Ping had dominated the young golfer demographics, but they were now following players like Tiger Woods, who was playing blade irons. Karsten's offset, cavity-backed irons had taken the market away from blades in the early '80s. So we developed a blade version of the i3 that was similar to the Eye 2, but smaller and didn't have offset except in the long irons. It was designed to be used by the better player. It also gave us that lead product in irons we were looking for, which I feel is like what the Corvette and Viper do for Chevrolet and Dodge. (I'm a car buff.)

Having a great product, however, doesn't make it sell today. So three years ago we set about on a program to educate the golf professional about our clubs. This really is much like what Karsten personally did years ago. Everywhere he went, he would teach people about our clubs and the importance of proper fitting. The program includes a fitting cart, but most of all, it is an educational program for our cart customers. Through the program, we have brought in over 3,000 professionals from all over the world to learn about Ping fitting and our company. In conjunction, I asked our leaders at Ping to make it possible for the fitting cart professional who placed an order on Monday to have a custom set built and delivered in time for his customer to play that weekend. Karsten's dedicated employees delivered 98 percent of the sets on time the first year of this program.

Throughout the '90s the golf bag business has grown and become a strong part of our business. It is great to see in competitions such as the NCAA Championship, whose players are not paid, the success Ping has had. Two years ago we had 100 percent of the bags in the NCAA Championship and in the last couple of Championships only seven of the 560 players were not using a Ping bag. This lead position was also achieved in the driver and iron counts this year.

The golf industry has been in a double-digit slump the last two years ('98, '99) due in large part to companies over-building and dumping product, into the marketplace. Ping, during these two years, has had double-digit growth and this year we are on track to have by far our biggest year ever. But on the horizon, the Royal and Ancient Golf Club of St. Andrews, which is the governing body of golf everywhere outside the United States and Mexico, has announced a possible ruling on metal woods of 15 degrees or less. I hope this does not turn into another groove-type issue.

In the latter part of 1999 I traveled a great deal introducing our new products. Much of the travel was with my son Andy. It was a very hectic schedule, but enjoyable as well. I was proud to see Andy be able to step up and handle some of the products and cover subjects I had missed as well. It reminded me of some of the product introductions Karsten and I did together. It wasn't until a golf journalist asked me about all of the miles I had traveled that I realized what I was doing was very much like what Karsten had done in his many world trips years before.

After the PGA National Golf Show in early February

this year, there was kind of a waiting period for Doug and me as we knew we'd done as much as we possibly could, but would not know if we had really succeeded until July. During this time before the golfing season began, there wasn't much more we could do on the marketing side.

Karsten's last two weeks before he left us were probably the best two weeks he'd had in his last two years. He seemed to be feeling better and was more alert. During this time he was able to see the successes that were starting to come with the woods and irons, much as the putter had done the year before. I could feel his satisfaction in knowing this. He also enjoyed tours of Moon Valley Country Club, which was in the process of renovation by long-time Ping employee Gary Hart and renowned golf course architect, Bob Cupp. Karsten was very happy to see Bob doing some of the things he had wanted to include when he redid the course in the '80s.

After Karsten's passing, I looked back at the time of his joining the Lord. He died on a Wednesday, which in the golf business is the day you make a big announcement; that is, you normally don't make it during a tournament but the day before. It was also just after the PGA Merchandise Show in Florida and the PGA Tour was in Los Angeles and would be heading to Tucson. I took the timing of my father's passing as his saying to me, "Nice job, John" and, "I'm leaving things in good hands!" Dad died suddenly in just a matter of minutes, as if God touched him and said, "Karsten, your work is done. It's time to come home to Me."

My mother told me of how my father had asked her to marry him, how he said he knew God had a plan for him, but didn't know what it was, and would she join him on the journey. Karsten's life has led me to a much greater understanding of Proverbs 3:5–6:

KARSTEN'S WAY

Trust in the Lord with all your heart,
and lean not on your own understanding;
In all your ways acknowledge Him,
And He shall direct your paths.

This is what guided my father's life and continues to guide the lives of our family.

We've started using nationally known consultants Bob Cottor and John Crosby of Family-Business Roundtable to assist us in planning for the next generation of the generations after that. They have been extremely effective in helping us work together as a family. My brothers and I have a goal to make sure we have the company in a position so the next generations can understand and effectively manage the business and keep it as Karsten always wanted it, a family business.

At the time of Karsten's death, there was still a question of whether we were over the hump. We had done well with the spring orders, but the real test would be the repeat orders. Now, that it is several months later, I can accept we've succeeded.

At a time when employee loyalty and retention is low nationwide, we have many long-time employees at our company. We have several employees working for us that were hired over thirty years ago, and forty that have been here twenty years or more. We consider them, as well as all of our employees, extended family. These people have stayed with us through the good times and the bad, and my family and I are so appreciative. Our goal for the future is to be the unquestioned leader in innovation, design, quality, and service in the golf industry. I know that our family, aided by this strong team, can accomplish our goal by pulling together and doing it Karsten's Way.

JOHN A. SOLHEIM

Appendix 1
BUSINESS LOCATIONS AND SUBSIDIARIES

Of the many places Karsten and Louise lived with their family of three sons and a daughter—Seattle, Fresno, San Diego, the Bay area south of San Francisco, upstate New York, and Phoenix—Karsten always talked of going back to live in the San Diego area someday.

San Diego, with its reputation for almost ideal year-round weather conditions, beckoned him. In the summer of 1965, as his hobby sideline of putter manufacturing was looking brighter every day just by word-of-mouth advertising, Karsten told Louise they should take a trip over there to look at possible sites for a business location someday. That "someday" was much nearer than either of them anticipated.

They spent a pleasant weekend following want-ad listings and visiting friends. But none of the listings appealed to Karsten, and they returned to Phoenix thinking there was plenty of time to make that kind of decision.

Then, in 1966, Karsten designed his Anser putter. Orders flooded into his small home shop, and it became necessary to look for a new place to make the putters.

Louise reasoned that zoning was important. They needed A-1 zoning, which was industrial, but could make do with C-4 zoning, which was commercial. They found an ad for a place with an unfinished concrete slab, situated near the freeway. It had the A-1 zoning they needed, but the owners did not want to sell. They wanted only to lease the property. This was unsatisfactory, because Karsten wanted to purchase the land for his growing business.

They continued to look and finally found a warehouse they could rent south of Bell Road on 32d Street. The zoning was C-4 and would allow them to assemble their putters. They put an $800 deposit on the building to cover the first and last months' rent and were ready to begin their move.

But that very evening they received a phone call from the people who owned the desirable property with the A-1 zoning. They were willing to construct a building on the slab, build to Karsten's specifications, and then give him an option to buy both that property and the lot next door.

Karsten and Louise didn't have to talk this over. It was the answer to their prayers, and the door was open for the beginning of Karsten Manufacturing Corporation. They forfeited the deposit on the warehouse C-4 location and began making plans for the move. Karsten drew up the plans for his new building, and in late summer of 1966 they moved into the specially designed 2,200-square-foot quarters.

Just at this time, however, General Electric told Karsten that he was to be transferred to Oklahoma City. Since he did not want to move to Oklahoma City, he and Louise decided it was time to devote full time to his growing club-making business.

By the first of 1967, orders for putters were pouring in, and it became necessary to hire more people to help fill them. It was at this time that their youngest son, John, decided to leave Arizona State University to help hire and train the new people for this growing business. Within a few months they had about fifteen employees, including Cathy Terrazzino, Kathy Shaurette, Bill Miller, John Keeney, Bob Driescher, Rick Hepler, Gilberto Peralta, John Otten, and Polly Hogg. Son Allan resigned from his job at GE and joined his father's new company, also.

A little less than one year later, the Solheims found that

their new building was already getting too small for the number of orders that were coming in. This prompted Karsten to begin drawing up plans for a warehouse type of building to be built on the back of the lot.

It was at just this time that Lee Richardson, the man who owned the property next door, contacted Karsten about purchasing his attractive 18,000-square-foot building. Richardson's business was manufacturing camera and telescope lenses for companies such as Disney and the Kitt Peak Observatory. He had just sold his company, which the new owners moved to California, and he wanted to dispose of the building.

Karsten's immediate reaction to the proposal was that he could not afford to do anything just then. And he didn't need to buy a building that large, because he really didn't need that much space.

However, another door was opening for Karsten Manufacturing, again at just the right time. Richardson asked Karsten to come over to see him so that they could talk about it.

That evening Karsten and Louise listened to Richardson's offer and agreed to his terms. Karsten assumed the existing mortgage on the building, and Richardson said he would carry a second mortgage. The only money that passed between the men was $38,000 for the existing machinery that Karsten could use in his club manufacturing. He also hired some of Richardson's employees, including several machinists and tool and dye makers and his accountant, Jeanette Fardy.

In May 1968, the transfer was made. In just one-and-one-half years, from late summer of 1966 to spring of 1968, the fledgling company had moved from a 2,200-square-foot building into 18,000 square feet.

This was an important time. The USGA had just declared Karsten's forged irons nonconforming because of their slight patented bend in the shaft. But Karsten was not deterred by this. He went back to the drawing board and began working on a new model, which he decided should be investment cast instead of forged. This method of making club heads was much more exact, allowing each club in the set to be balanced and matched. This enabled him to incorporate his heel-toe and perimeter weighting more efficiently. These new models were called the Karsten I irons and started being shipped in late 1969.

Then it was 1971. Karsten Manufacturing was becoming known all over the world, first for its putters and then for the dull-finished irons with the cavity in the back of the club heads. About that time, the owner of an investment-cast foundry in Phoenix approached Karsten about buying his plant. (Karsten was having all the heads cast in foundries in California.) The owner approached him several times, but Karsten said he had his hands full. Finally the man told him that the least he could do was make him an offer for the foundry.

Thinking it over, Karsten could definitely see advantages in owning his own foundry, such as better quality control, elimination of the middleman, and better control over his clubs. He had seen clubs show up that had no serial numbers on them.

Finally, in 1972, he decided to make an offer for the foundry but only on condition that the then current manager, George Ball, and other employees stayed on. This condition was acceptable. Karsten asked George what he wanted to name the foundry. Since George was an avid fisherman, he suggested calling the newly acquired plant "Dolphin, Inc."

And so the first of many acquisitions was accomplished.

Also about that time, Karsten was planning an addition to the Richardson building. In the four years that he had owned the building, they had needed more space. He decided to make a two-story office section in the front part of the plant. The new addition was ready to be occupied in 1973.

More growth lay ahead. The popularity of the putters was growing worldwide. Mark McCormack, agent for Jack Nicklaus in England and Gary Player in South Africa, approached Karsten Manufacturing for distribution rights to putters. Since Nicklaus was under contract to Slazenger, all the putters for England had to be assembled by Slazenger and carry their name. This partnership, commencing in 1967, lasted for about three years.

But because the demand for Ping products was growing so fast, and Karsten was beginning to make his own irons, he decided he did not want outside involvement in this part of his business. He felt the need to start his own company in the United Kingdom, so he hired Roy Freeman, the accountant who had been working for the previous distributor. It was the beginning of an international company, which Karsten named Karsten (U.K.) Ltd.

Karsten and Roy hit it off right away, and he was so pleased with Roy's integrity that he gave him a 5 percent interest in the new company. Roy and his wife, Patricia, rented a little shop with a small window and began the new business. Its growth forced them to move two or three times in the next few years. As need dictated, Roy added new employees to help with orders. Located in Gainsborough, Lincolnshire, that little company now includes 100 employees, who oversee the distribution and assembling of Ping products in the United Kingdom and Europe.

Then, in 1984, Roy showed Karsten a wonderful piece of property not far from town and also near a golf course. Karsten decided to acquire this. A few years later Karsten (U.K.) also bought the golf course. Later he built a new clubhouse and added another eighteen-hole golf course.

In 1974, an opportunity had arisen to purchase Sonee

Heat Treating facility, managed by Terry Joseph. Karsten had used this company in the manufacture of his clubs and could see the advantage of ownership. Sonee was added to the growing list of subsidiaries.

Then word reached him of a golf-ball company for sale in Michigan. He decided to buy the machinery, hire the manager, Buzz Piechowski, and move the product to Phoenix. In order to do this, he would have to construct another building behind the present Richardson building. By 1975, the new ball-making company was ready to go into operation.

In twenty years' time, Karsten owned every building on 21st Avenue from Peoria Avenue to Desert Cove. It had been a huge transition from the little shop on the corner of 21st and Desert Cove.

In 1980, the Iran hostage situation caused him concern. He remembered how World War Two had shut down the aluminum cookware business, and he was not going to be caught like that again. If our country was to go to war, it would most surely mean that all golf-club production would cease. Manufacturing efforts would again need to focus on products to help the war effort. So Karsten began buying big machines that could be used to make precision parts for government work. His oldest son, Karsten Louis, played a large part in the acquisition of these machines. This was the beginning of Karsten Engineering. A building was constructed especially for Karsten Engineering in early 1980.

The machines were a source of pride for Karsten. He loved taking visitors on tours to show them the huge pieces of equipment that could make such precise parts. Today KE makes precision parts for intricate guidance systems.

During all those years, the Solheims loved to return to their roots in Seattle. In 1973 they bought a home on the waterfront in Suquamish and would frequently travel there to soak up the beautiful Pacific Northwest scenery, visit family, and look up old friends. Karsten's two sisters, Elaine Solheim and Marjorie Korsak, live near there.

Then, in 1983, during one visit to Suquamish, they were approached to buy a piece of property not far from their home. It was a parcel of commercial real estate that included a hardware store, plumbing shop, and beauty salon. Soon Karsten was having plans drawn up to develop the little shopping center.

Over the next eight years he added a restaurant, service station, and grocery store, plus several spaces that could be leased to local businesses. But Karsten, who had been so successful in the design, manufacture, and distribution of golf clubs, found the shopping-center business difficult to manage. He was at the end of a long and successful career, and he decided that his interests at home needed his full attention. Currently the center, Suquamish Village Square, is listed for sale.

OTHER UNDERTAKINGS

Manufacturing clubs and fighting the legal battle were not all that Karsten undertook in the 1980s. The Moon Valley golf course, where the Solheims lived, was going downhill. The members who owned the club were losing money and didn't have the capital needed to construct new greens and install an updated irrigation system. The clubhouse needed renovating, and the wait staff had been wearing the same uniforms for about five years. Rumor had it that the members were considering filling in the lakes and selling the property for condominiums.

Besides the fact that the Solheims loved living on a golf course, they worried what two or three hundred new families moving into condos would do to the value of the property in the area. Louise and Karsten talked and prayed about it and eventually made an offer to buy Moon Valley from the members.

The offer was put up for a vote among the membership of the country club, and 72 percent approved. The minority, however, small and seemingly insignificant as their numbers were, did not take the decision lightly. They formed an association designed to hold the Solheims to the promises they had made about upgrading the place. Their bylaws called for the group to remain intact for several years, making sure the Solheims spent enough money to bring Moon Valley back up to snuff. Within a year, the little band of resistance fizzled as Karsten and Louise used their best ideas and staff, including the mind of their son Lou, in overhauling the entire operation.

The Solheims poured millions into Moon Valley, making it suitable for use for pro events and increasing the membership. The clubhouse was remodeled three times, being enlarged each time. A fitness center was added, greens were redone, a new irrigation system was installed, the course remodeled, a par-3 course added. Even the wait staff uniforms were new.

Appendix 2
AWARDS

N umerous statewide and national awards have been presented to Karsten Solheim and his corporation. They include:

Honorary Thunderbird (Special Events Committee of the Phoenix Chamber of Commerce and sixty-two-year sponsor of the Phoenix Open), January 1985

Induction into the Phoenix Business Hall of Fame, January 1987

Arizona Association of Industries Award, 1987. Presented by Paul Harvey.

The American Jewish Committee Human Relations Award, 1990.

Inducted into the Scandinavian Hall of Fame at the Norsk Hostfest, October 1991

Recipient of the Patty Berg Award, to reward outstanding contributions to women's golf, 1991

"E" Star Award for continued excellence in exporting, 1991

Creation of the Solheim Lifetime Achievement Award as a Sports Executive, presented annually by the March of Dimes, 1992

Honorary Doctor of Science degree from Arizona State University, December 18, 1992

Golfweek Magazine Golf Industry Father of the Year, June 1994

National Golf Foundation Golf Family of the Year, November 1994

LPGA Commissioner's Award, November 1994

First Annual Homeward Bound Golf Charity Leadership Award, 1994

Metropolitan Golf Writer's Association Family of the Year, May 1995

PGA of America Ernie Sabayrac Award for Lifetime Contributions to the Golf Industry, September 1996

Honorary Grand Marshal of the Fiesta Bowl Parade, December 1996

Golf Industry News Europe Lifetime Achievement Award, 1999

Ford Lifetime Achievement Award, June 1999

One of the 100 most famous, fascinating and influential University of Washington Alumni of the Century, 1999

Top 25 Architects and Builders of Arizona Sports, 1999

Enjoyable recognition was bestowed upon Karsten Solheim and his wife, Louise, on a return visit to the White House in 1995 with the victorious United States LPGA Solheim Cup team. In addition to an Oval Office meeting with President Bill Clinton, the trip included a Congressional reception on Capitol Hill.

In 1996, Solheim became the fifth recipient of the prestigious Ernie Sabayrac Award, presented by the PGA of America for lifetime contributions to the golf industry.

Appendix 3
TIMELINE

Karsten Solheim, a General Electric mechanical engineer, invents putter in his Redwood City, Calif., garage; names it PING because of sound it makes when striking a ball.

First PING putter win by John Barnum at PGA Tour's Cajun Classic.

World Cup is televised from Japan, where top players use PING putters. Orders for PING putters, which are still being built in family garage, continue to grow.

1959   **1961** **1962**   **1965**

Patent filed on March 23, 1959 for PING 1A putter.

Karsten moves family to Phoenix; continues to make PING putter in garage. Heel-toe weighting concept of putters begins to catch on as putters earn reputation for forgiveness on mis-hit putts.

Karsten experiments with heel-toe weighted irons by milling out a cavity in forged iron.

Anser putter is designed as an "answer" to competitors' putters. Louise Solheim, Karsten's wife, named putter after encouraging him to leave out the "w" to help name fit on toe of putter.

USGA outlaws all PING clubs—except Anser putter—because of slight bend in shaft under grip. Claims it gives unfair advantage.

PING introduces KI iron. A perimeter weighted, investment cast iron made from 17-4ph stainless steel.

1966   **1967**   **1969**

Karsten resigns position at GE to build PING golf equipment full time. Incorporates Karsten Manufacturing Corporation and moves from family garage to company's present location in north Phoenix, Arizona.

Anser patent granted March 21, 1967

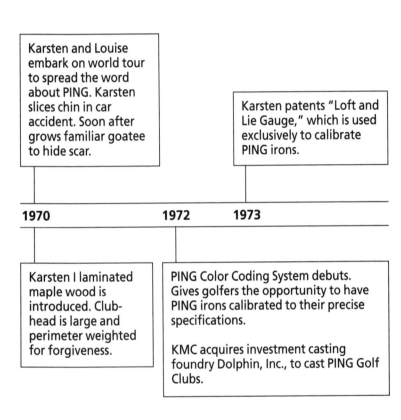

Karsten and Louise embark on world tour to spread the word about PING. Karsten slices chin in car accident. Soon after grows familiar goatee to hide scar.

Karsten patents "Loft and Lie Gauge," which is used exclusively to calibrate PING irons.

1970 **1972** **1973**

Karsten I laminated maple wood is introduced. Club-head is large and perimeter weighted for forgiveness.

PING Color Coding System debuts. Gives golfers the opportunity to have PING irons calibrated to their precise specifications.

KMC acquires investment casting foundry Dolphin, Inc., to cast PING Golf Clubs.

KMC acquires Sonee, Inc., a heat treating facility. Heat treating of PING irons and putters ensures consistency and quality and allows clubs to be adjusted for lost and lie.

PING tops putter count at U.S. Open and British Open for first time to begin current streak of being the top putter choice for 20 straight years.

PING EYE iron is introduced. Patented "eye" shape in cavity helps improve feel and consistency of club.

PING professional Jerilyn Britz wins U.S. Women's Open playing PING Eye irons.

1975   **1976**   **1979**

First PING Man developed. Engineered and built in-house, the mechanical golfer is designed with shoulder rotation and a free-moving wrist to precisely simulate the human swing.

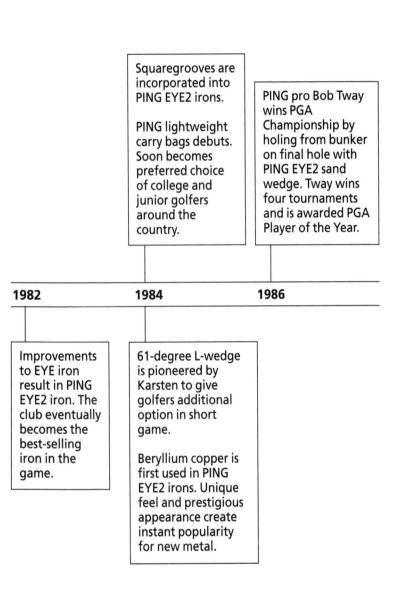

Squaregrooves are incorporated into PING EYE2 irons.

PING lightweight carry bags debuts. Soon becomes preferred choice of college and junior golfers around the country.

PING pro Bob Tway wins PGA Championship by holing from bunker on final hole with PING EYE2 sand wedge. Tway wins four tournaments and is awarded PGA Player of the Year.

1982   **1984**   **1986**

Improvements to EYE iron result in PING EYE2 iron. The club eventually becomes the best-selling iron in the game.

61-degree L-wedge is pioneered by Karsten to give golfers additional option in short game.

Beryllium copper is first used in PING EYE2 irons. Unique feel and prestigious appearance create instant popularity for new metal.

Ping putters win all four modern majors in one year—the only putter in history to accomplish this feat.

President Ronald Reagan honors Karsten at White House for export excellence.

Solheim Cup is founded. The biennial match pits the top United States women professionals against Europe's finest in a Ryder Cup-style event. U.S. wins inaugural match 11.5–4.5.

| 1987 | 1988 | 1989 | 1990 |

Anser2 putter is used to win PGA Championship to mark the 25th major PING putter win.

PING pro Mark Calcavercchia wins British Open at Royal Troon in playoff. A PING EYE2 beryllium copper five-iron shot on the final hole in regulation earns him "Shot of the Year" honors from *Golf Magazine*.

Bag stand is introduced as an option on PING lightweight carry bags. Eventually becomes standard on all PING carry bags.

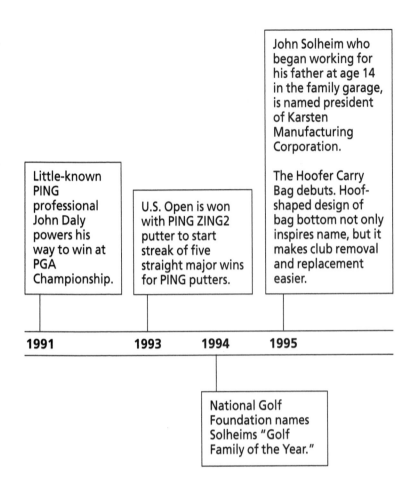

John Solheim who began working for his father at age 14 in the family garage, is named president of Karsten Manufacturing Corporation.

The Hoofer Carry Bag debuts. Hoof-shaped design of bag bottom not only inspires name, but it makes club removal and replacement easier.

Little-known PING professional John Daly powers his way to win at PGA Championship.

U.S. Open is won with PING ZING2 putter to start streak of five straight major wins for PING putters.

1991

1993 **1994** **1995**

National Golf Foundation names Solheims "Golf Family of the Year."

Cushin Selective Filtering Insert is introduced. Inserted in all steel shafts, the Cushin improves feel by reducing vibrations that occur at impact.

Isopür insert is developed for PING putters. Putters are distinguished by brand identifying, clear inset which provides "true feel" and feedback.

PING Inc., a wholly owned subsidiary of Karsten Manufacturing is formed.

1996   1997   1998   1999

PING ISI irons are introduced in nickel.

PGA of America honors Karsten Solheim with Ernie Sabayrac Award for lifetime contributions to golf.

PING TiSI driver debuts as largest custom-fit driver in golf. First year on market is highlighted by wins at Men's and Women's U.S. Amateur Championships as well as wins around the world.

PING Wrx, a development center for new products and processes, is created to further advance PING's commitment to advancing golf club technology.

Putter wins top 1800. Wins of The Masters and British Open give PING putters 47 majors all time. Every player at Men's and Women's NCAA Division 1 Championships carries a PING bag.

Appendix 4
LETTERS

The following are excerpts from letters Karsten's family received at the time of his death.

Karsten had the best work ethic of anyone I have ever known. He was a tireless worker and loved to go to work.

Karsten was the most hospitable person I have ever known.

Respect for the common man was a characteristic of Karsten's. He gave many people jobs through the years, who were needy, new in town, needed another chance, immigrants, etc.

Karsten was so generous and giving. On a Christmas Eve day one year, Karsten and Louise went downtown and made plans to purchase a homeless shelter for the Solheim Foundation because people were going to be evicted soon. That was what kind of heart he had.

Karsten and Louise will go down as philanthropists extraordinaire. They have made many gifts of buildings, golf courses, mission projects, in order to help the community, the church, the world, but they would consider none as important as those which will further the gospel of Jesus Christ.

Sunday was a wonderful day of worship and fellowship, but each day of the week the open Bible was on the kitchen table. It was read, discussed, applied to life's situations—a strength and refuge in times of trouble, a guide for each day. Many people have benefited from Karsten's strong testimony of faith. But his commitment to the Lord and the work done in HIS behalf will have eternal value.

BILL AND JUDY GARRETT
Longtime friends, Bill is a former PGA player

Karsten was a man of great integrity and devotion. We are honored to have known him. I could go on and on telling about the kind, gentle spirit that Karsten showed his employees and tour staff and about his generosity.

DOUG TEWELL
Two-time winner on PGA Senior Tour

He was certainly kind and generous to me, but then he was to everyone. But he was something far more than that. I think he was a beacon, an example. He showed me that it was possible to be truly good, whilst still being successful. He showed me that it was possible to combine honesty, integrity, generosity, kindness and humility with being a giant in his field.

He quite literally changed my life . . . he taught me something of more value than a million gold-plated putters. He taught me right from wrong in business.

HUGH MURRAY
Founder and Chief Executive of Fenman, Ltd.
(Great Britain)

To be in his presence however, was a special and inspiring experience. Karsten was an honorable and generous man of impeccable character, in addition to being a genius.

J. WAYNE RUMBLE
General Manager, Brunswick Golf, retired

I also had the greatest respect for his courage, faith and integrity. I believe that Karsten was held in the highest regard by his peers in the industry because of his uncompromising integrity.

DAVE, SHARON, SUNDAY AND JED WALTERS
General Manager, Santa Fe Country Club

I have always said that Karsten was ahead of his time. I remember seeing him at a PGA show in Florida several years ago, after his patents had run out. I remarked how every club manufacturer was copying his concept, and he said that he was very flattered that they thought enough of his ideas to do their own thing.

ANDY (ANDREA) FISCHER
Former LPGA Tour Player

If you are interested in information
about other books written from a
biblical perspective, please write
to the following address:

Northfield Publishing
215 West Locust Street
Chicago, IL 60610